GHOSTS
OF THE BAY

THE FAMOUS INSIDE ROUTE

TO

PARRY SOUND

AND

PARRY HARBOR

—|THE STEAMER|—

GEORGIANA

Will leave Penetanguishene, 7 a.m., Midland, at 8.30, every MONDAY, WEDNESDAY and FRIDAY for Parry Sound and Parry Harbor, and Parry Sound at 7 a.m., Parry Harbor at 7.30 a.m. every TUESDAY, THURSDAY and SATURDAY for Penetanguishene and Midland, connecting with the N. & N.W. Railway at Penetanguishene for Toronto, which city can be reached the same evening. On departure of N. & N. W. Railway train from Penetanguishene she will run to Midland, arriving at 6 p.m. and will there await the arrival of the Mid. train, returning then to Penetanguishene. Parties leaving Toronto at 5 p.m. will reach Parry Sound or Parry Harbor the following afternoon.

The Steamer has been specially adapted to run the South, or Inside Channel between the above-mentioned Ports; and when the public are made aware that by this route they may enjoy a three-fold benefit over any other route viz. an all daylight trip, a short and safe passage, thoroughly secure from all danger of tempest, or the even worse bane of sea sickness; and lastly, the enjoyment of a route which will enable them to see the grandest and most fairy-like scenery in the world, coupled with a sense of security that must gain the confidence of the most timid—the owners feel assured that they have only to induce the public to try this route once in order to secure their patronage.

Special arrangements have been made whereby Tourists to the numerous Islands that lay on this route can be conveyed to their destination, together with their camping outfits, and left on any island they may desire and can be brought in again on any of the steamer's regular trips.

Parties can procure cheap Return Tickets from Toronto to Penetanguishene or Midland.

Rates for Freight and Passengers lower than any other route. Special rates to families moving into the great Parry Sound Free Grant District, and for Lumbermen's Supplies.

For all particulars, apply to

J. PRENTICE,	M. McLENNAN,	H. F. SWITZER,
Parry Harbor.	Parry Sound.	Midland.

or, C. BECK & CO., Penetanguishene.

Ghosts
of the
Bay

A Guide to the History of Georgian Bay

Written by
Russell Floren
Andrea Gutsche

Edited by
Barbara Chisholm

Editor: Barbara D. Chisholm
Cover illustration and design: James Flaherty
Typesetting and design: Lynx Images Inc.
1st edition, July 1994
2nd edition, October 1994
3rd printing, May 1995
4th printing, April 1998

Printed and bound in Canada by Metrolitho Inc.

Canadian Cataloguing in Publication Data

Floren, Russell, 1965-
    Ghosts of the Bay: a guide to the history of Georgian Bay

Includes bibliographical references and index.
ISBN 0-9698427-3-2

1.Georgian Bay (Ont. :Bay) - History.
2. Georgian Bay Region (Ont.)- History.   I. Gutsche,
Andrea, 1964-   . II. Chisholm, Barbara, 1932-
III. Title.

FC3095.G3F5 1994   971.3'15   C94-932512-0
F1059.G3F5 1994

Dr. W.R.F. Luke, 1918

This Book and accompanying film is dedicated to all Georgian Bay adventurers and to the one who helped me understand the Bay: my grandfather, Dr. William Russel Ferguson Luke. I can still hear him singing opera as he rows around Primrose Island.

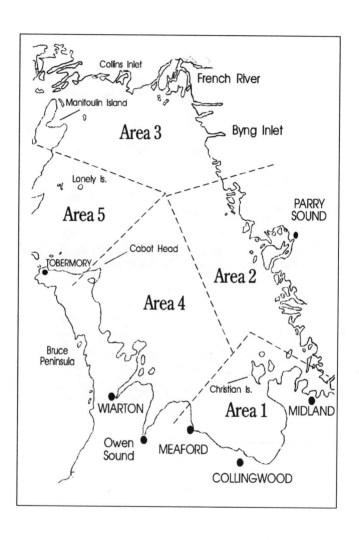

Table of Contents

Notes about this book and maps.

When trying to locate the sites in this book it is necessary to obtain proper maps and charts for the relevant areas. These will direct you to the sites and away from shoals. Many shipwrecks are marked on the charts. The maps in this book are to help the reader gain a sense of the area and are not to be used for navigation. Information and portions of charts are reproduced by permission of the Canadian Hydrographic Service, Ottawa. The nautical chart portions reproduced in this book are not to be used for navigation.

Every effort has been made to make this book accurate, informative, and useful. While we have scoured the Bay for stories and interesting information, we do not claim to be doing an exhaustive historical treatment. In condensing complex histories, we are aware of the risk of misrepresenting situations, and hope that our portrayals are found to be fair.

Exploring Georgian Bay is not a simple task, it requires a thorough knowledge of boating, navigation, and, in some cases, diving. Readers should be confident they have the skills with which to safely enjoy their exploration of the Bay, or they are travelling with somone who does. When going to these sites you do so at your own risk. Lynx Images Inc. takes no responsibility for what might befall you. We have made every effort to note when a site is on or near private property and when permission is required in order to visit a site. Divers must be certified. And we can't stress enough that respect and common sense should always travel with you when on the Bay.

We welcome new stories, updates, information and corrections for subsequent editions. Please write: Lynx Images, P.O. Box 5961, Station A., Toronto, Ontario, M5W 1P4.

Preface

Georgian Bay. Her moods and landscapes are diverse and compelling. Her shoals are many and tricky. Her winds and waters can be unpredictable and even capricious... she defies simple description.

I have summered on Georgian Bay my entire life. When I was young, my grandfather taught me about the Bay, most importantly to respect her. He showed me how to navigate her shoals and pay heed to her winds. But I always felt there was something more to the Bay than her physical presence – something in the wind, in a storm, in the darkness of night.... This feeling began with my visits to the abandoned Copperhead Hotel on an island close to our cottage. I would row over and stare into her dark windows, convinced that spirits were peering back at me.

During the 1920s and 1930s she was a popular resort, offering important services not only to her visitors but to those who lived and vacationed around her. But times changed, and soon the Copperhead was no longer the heart of the community. A few years of neglect wore her down. During my youth, she stood there, battered yet defiant against Georgian Bay's brutal storms and scorching sun. The peeling wallpaper could only whisper of her former grandeur, and now only the wind touched the yellowed keys of her piano.

In the spring of 1988, we rounded the channel to find the Copperhead gone. I wondered about the spirits that inhabited those windswept rooms. Where did they go? Would anyone remember them? And what of all the other spirits on Georgian Bay — were they also lost to places long ago abandoned?

Ghosts of the Bay, both the book and the film, is a journey in search of these spirits, a journey to rediscover Georgian Bay's remarkable history: her shipwrecks, ghost towns, legends, and myth. It is a tribute to those who are forgotten, to those who dared to make a life on this unpredictable Bay.

As fierce as Georgian Bay can be, she is also fragile and must be treated with care. When you travel to the places in this book, please have respect for the sites and for the residents who live near them. Leave locations the way you found them. And let yourself be inspired, be touched by the voices in the wind and the waves. These are the voices that speak to me, these are the Ghosts of the Bay.

Russell Floren
July 1994

Introduction

When we first began this project, we had our doubts. We had taken a good look at a Georgian Bay map and thought, "no way." How could we possibly include everything there is to know about this unusual, enormous body of water in just one book. Each diverse shore merits its own story. As we researched, we were astonished by the overwhelming amount of rich material that had seemingly been tucked away for centuries. It was as if Georgian Bay were guarding her secrets, saving them for the curious, those who looked past her present-day scenic attractions to her spirited heritage, once alive with adventure, enterprise, hope, excitement, and, of course, a little intrigue. We were hooked.

Even after years of exploration by boat, foot, dive tank, library, and museum, there is still much left to be learned about this fascinating place. We are confident, however, that we have put together an easy-to-follow "story-telling" guide to some of the hidden sights of this "Sixth Great Lake." We hope it encourages you to discover stories to add to her richly layered history and to broaden your appreciation of her.

So take the book along as you enjoy the Bay. Look for the shipwrecks tucked into her dark, shadowy waters; discover the ghost towns, now cloaked in the heavy foliage of an ever-encroaching forest. But most importantly, listen for the voices of her people – bold, confident, determined – lost in the cries of the gulls and the whispering wind. You'll be hooked, too.

In The Beginning

Formed over 100,000 years ago, the Great Lakes and Georgian Bay were born from a succession of massive forces. The area was once submerged under a vast, warm coral sea. Then, great mountains of Arctic ice advanced, slowly grinding their way back and forth across the continent, scraping and gouging out a galaxy of islands and shoals, and flooding their path with meltwaters. Much of this turbulent birth is still visible along the shores of the Bay.

Georgian Bay's terrain changes as quickly as do her weather and spirit. Her southern shore is rimmed with beaches that are backed by farms and orchards, wild meadows and hardwood groves. Her eastern shore is broken up by numerous inlets and dotted with tens of thousands of treeless islands and pink granite shoals, while the jagged limestone cliffs of the Bruce Peninsula define her western shore. Part of the Niagara Escarpment, the Bruce is relatively flat on top and covered with fertile soil. Conifers and birch abound. In startling contrast is the smooth, bare rock of the north shore.   Here, the Canadian Precambrian Shield has relented only to juniper and blueberry bushes, patches of moss and lichen, and the occasional gnarled scrub pine or cedar tree. It is breathtakingly beautiful yet treacherous and demanding.

As for the weather - on a given day, the Bay can offer blistering heat or finger-numbing north winds; placid, mirror-like waters or stomach-churning waves; great deep stretches of open water, perfect for carefree boating, or perilous archipelagos of hidden shoals and islands, waiting to wreak havoc on the hull of any boat. The Bay's diversity, great size, and positioning, command respect. 120 miles long and 50 miles wide (192km by 80km), she runs southeast to northwest exposed to fierce winds from the Great Lakes.

She has borne many names. The Ojibwa Indians called her "Spirit Lake." To the Hurons she was "Lake of Attigouatan." Explorer, colonist, and Governor of New France Samuel de Champlain wrote of "*La Mer Douce*" (the sweet water sea) in his journal – the first record of Georgian Bay – in 1615. Two hundred years later, chartmaker Captain William Fitzwilliam Owen of the Royal Navy labelled it "Lake Manitoulin" meaning home of the

Great Spirit. In the early 1820s, the Bay was decreed to be part of Lake Huron, and British surveyor Lieutenant Henry Bayfield named her "Georgian Bay" after George IV, King of Great Britain and Ireland. And so she has remained.

Iroquois (right) and Algonkin (left)

Early Inhabitants

Archaeological evidence suggests that hunting and gathering Indians lived on the Bay as early as 9,000 B.C.. The population was comprised of two linguistic groups. To the north were the Algonkian-speaking peoples (Ojibwa, Chippewa, Algonkin, and Ottawa,) who traded with their Iroquoian-speaking southern neighbours (Iroquois,

Ouendate or Huron, Tobacco or Petun, and Neutral.) Champlain estimated the number of Indians to be 20,000.

Much has been written about the Bay's Ouendate people. The Ouendate (or Wyandot or Wendat) means "Islanders/Dwellers on the Peninsula." They were one of the first tribes to have contact with European traders. To the French they were known as "Hurons" because of their hair style, which they thought resembled that of a wild boar (*hure*). There is no record of what the Ouendate called the French. What we do know of the Ouendate come's from Champlain's diary, the numerous stories in the *Jesuit Relations*, and the findings of archaeologist William Jury and his team in the 1950s.

The Huron settled on the southern shores and islands of Georgian Bay in Huronia, or Ouendake (Wendake) which means "Land Apart." The Bear, Cord, Rock, and Deer clans of the Huron Nation spread out over more than twenty villages from Cedar Point to Thunder Beach to Orr Lake and Tiny Marsh. Here they lived a rather sedentary life, farming thousands of acres of beans, squash, pumpkin, and corn, and trading with other tribes across the Great Lakes.

The Huron were more than farmers, however. They and other Iroquoian-speaking peoples were unique in their political, social, and religious organization. In fact, the Iroquois influenced many European philosophers, and both Canada and the United States chose to adopt the Iroquoian system of three levels of government — local or municipal, state or provincial, and federal. Socially, the Huron lived a comparatively free life, emphasizing good behaviour, modesty, loyalty, consideration, and fun. They enjoyed a sexual freedom that would later greatly upset the Jesuits. There was no physical punishment of children, and the only two crimes to incur severe penalties were theft and murder. The Huron believed in the *oki* (spirit) of the moon, which governed their souls, and the *oki* of the sun, which governed the living. They were risk takers who enjoyed gambling, and they were fiercely competitive, playing often bloody games of lacrosse. The only other violence erupted when the Huron had the occasional dispute over trade routes with the Iroquois to the south (in the area now known as upstate New York.) Overall, life was good. That would change all too soon.

The Huron were sophisticated merchants and traders, and on one of their trading expeditions to the St. Lawrence region, they met their first Europeans, the French. From Champlain they learned of his eagerness to strengthen trading ties with the native peoples. He suggested the French should send a young man to live with the Huron for a year to explore the area, to learn the Indian ways and to gain their trust. In exchange, a young Huron would travel with Champlain to France. A deal was made. The young Huron, Savignon, would be the first Huron to set foot in France.

In 1610, a few Huron travelled back from New France to Huronia via the French River with the first European to see the area, Etienne Brulé. He was an unlikely diplomat, this boy-man of eighteen years, who had left his peasant home in Paris at age sixteen for a better life in New France. He was confident, energetic, tough, and burdened little by religion, patriotism, or conscience. His dark good looks made him quite a ladies man. He quickly took to the Huron way of life.

After a year of total immersion in the Huron culture, Brulé met Champlain and "the exchange student" Savignon, near Montreal. Champlain was surprised at the change in Brulé, who was dressed in Indian garb and was now more fluent in the Indian dialects than in French. Clearly, Brulé had enjoyed himself much more than had Savignon, who reported that Paris was a savage and brutal society which allowed its people to beg in the streets, and condoned the spanking of children. But Savignon also told elaborate stories of the exotic, magical things he had seen such as a clock and the French king's "rolling golden cabin" drawn by eight moose without horns.

Champlain & Brulé meet with Huron.

The Huron were pleased with Brulé and invited him to continue living with them. He returned to Huronia and stayed for many years, acting as Champlain's agent. When Champlain visited the Bay in 1615, Brulé was his interpreter and guide. Champlain had come to Huronia to aid the Hurons in an offensive against the Iroquois. The Iroquois had been repeatedly raiding the Huron in protest of the Huron alliance with the French, and the Huron decided to retaliate with the help of their new allies. As they set out for Iroquois country, Champlain sent Brulé south to gather more support. This was the last he would see of Brulé for a long time, as the Frenchman simply disappeared into the forest. Without reinforcements, Champlain's attack against the Iroquois was a failure. Badly wounded, he spent the winter in Huronia before returning to New France. Brulé eventually resurfaced, full of near-death-escape-from-the-Iroquois stories. He, too, rested for a year with the Huron then continued his explorations. He was believed to be the first European to reach the North Channel and Lake Superior. Brulé eventually returned to Huronia to settle among the Indians.

But it was not a peaceful ending for Monsieur Brulé, no matter which story you believe. It is said that he was murdered in Huronia in 1633 for his disloyalty to Champlain and France. Champlain felt that Brulé's patriotism was a little "thin" - especially in 1629 when Brulé helped the British in an attempt to invade New France. Champlain voiced his dissatisfaction to the Huron, who could not abide disloyalty. Another version suggests that Brulé was killed because he traded with Indians along

Lake Ontario, cutting into the monopoly held by a Huron chief. A third story states he was killed in a fight over a Huron woman.

In his diary, the Jesuit missionary Jean De Brébeuf spoke of seeing the site where Brulé was buried, along with his rifle, swords, knives, and a few copper goods. The grave is believed to be in the area of the yet undiscovered Toanche (the main village of the Huron Bear Nation - not the present-day community) somewhere near Thunder Beach. Evidence suggests many possible locations for Toanche, but until further research is concluded, the authentic site, and the truth of Brulé's burial, will remain a mystery.

Jesuit Missionary, Jean de Brébeuf

The Bay Is Opened To All

Fast on the heels of the first French explorers came the first French missionaries. Their goal was not only to spread Christianity and create an entirely new French Catholic society but also to further strengthen France's trading bonds with the Indians. The first to arrive in 1615 was Father Joseph Le Caron of the Recollets (the Grey Robes) followed by Brother Gabriel Sagard in 1623. According to Sagard's journal, converting the natives was not as easy task. He had great trouble expressing the concepts of his religion in languages that did not contain words for angels, paradise, hell, and temptation. But the missionaries did not give up. In 1626, the Jesuits (or The Black Robes) sent Jean de Brébeuf to Huronia. He was a tall man in black robes, an intellect and visionary, fluent in American Indian languages and an authority on Indian customs and character. He stayed until 1629, when he was called back to New France. During his second trip to Huronia in 1632, he established a small mission on the banks of the Wye River. His aim was to teach and learn from the Huron, and to save as many Indian souls as possible, not only from the Devil but also from the small pox epidemic that was decimating the population.

Following Champlain's death in 1635, he was replaced at Huronia by Charles-Jacques Huault de Montmagny – a paranoid man driven by missionary zeal to convert the "heathen Indians" at any cost. Brébeuf was replaced by Father Jerome Lalemant, who believed Huronia was "a land of demons". So different from the level-headed Champlain, and the compassionate Brébeuf, the two new men signalled a change in philosophy. This would be the first of many tragedies to befall Huronia.

Missionaries were not the only Europeans interested in the native communities. Explorers saw the Indians succeeding in the fur trade. Soon canoes loaded down with furs were being paddled by both Europeans and Indians. These early fur traders, like the Frenchmen Médart Chouart de Groseilliers and Pierre Esprit Radisson, were called *coureurs de bois* (runners of the woods). They were independent adventurers, traders, and explorers. In 1662 a new route to Hudson Bay via the Great Lakes was discovered, dramatically changing the profile of the fur trade. Wealthy British businessmen sought backing for their plan to trade by ship into Hudson Bay. Shortly thereafter, the Hudson Bay Company was formed.

One of the first to prosper in the booming fur trade was Alexander Henry, who arrived at Georgian Bay in 1761. He spent ten years becoming one of the most successful traders on the Great Lakes then decided to move west to explore the abundance of furs in Saskatchewan. He joined efforts with three other men and formed the North West Company which soon dominated the Montreal fur trade. *Coureurs de bois* were replaced by *voyageurs* – canoemen in the service of one of the big trading companies whose job it was to move goods from Montreal to the western posts and to return laden with furs. A huge grid of relatively safe trade routes developed across the Great Lakes. More and more people settled around the fur trading posts and by the early 1800s, other settlements sprouted up, rapidly growing into villages and towns. Land was cleared, crops were planted, and domesticated animals shipped in. Entrepreneurs began to take advantage of the abundance of raw materials. Before long, the lumber and fishing industries were booming. Railroads and shipyards were built. Wiarton, Owen Sound, Collingwood, Midland, Parry Sound, and French River became crucial harbour towns and industrial centres, bustling with prosperity. The Bay's shores were dotted with grain silos, lumber mills, shipyards, rail terminals, and hotels, and her waters carried great freight and passenger vessels. Some of the luckier ships are now proudly displayed in museums around the Bay, while others took their secrets to their watery graves.

Ironically, the progress that made this region come alive also led to its demise. When most of the fish were caught, most of the trees cut, and when the automobile became the preferred mode of transportation, the fishing, lumber, and shipping industries declined. The Bay had one last resource to offer, one that could not be exported – herself. People began coming to the Bay to *enjoy* her alluring water, land, and air. And they came in the hundreds. Once again the Bay's shores hummed with activity - luxury hotels, summer homes, and cottages. Her waters were dotted with passenger cruisers, sailboats, motorboats, canoes, rowboats and anything else that could float. The influx continues today. Some are drawn to the neon attractions of Wasaga Beach, a few to the solitude of the Mink Islands, all come to enjoy the Bay's timeless beauty.

Amidst all the comings and goings Georgian Bay remains a constant. She carries the secrets of the hardy men and women who have been drawn here before, leaving only remnants of their myriad triumphs and failures. When we no longer need her, when she is no longer practical or useful, we move on. But Georgian Bay gradually takes back what is hers. Our footprints stay for a time, then she washes them away.

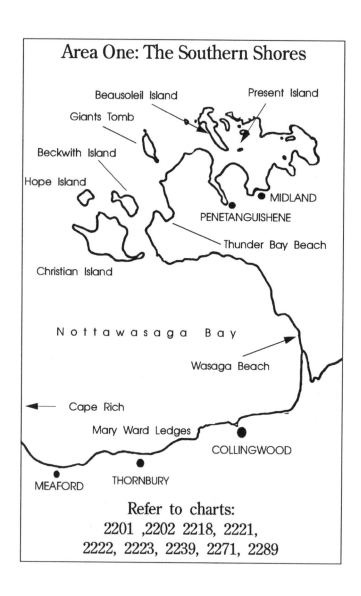

Area One: The Southern Shores

Beausoleil Island

Present Island

Giants Tomb

Beckwith Island

Hope Island

MIDLAND

PENETANGUISHENE

Thunder Bay Beach

Christian Island

N o t t a w a s a g a   B a y

Wasaga Beach

Cape Rich

Mary Ward Ledges

COLLINGWOOD

MEAFORD

THORNBURY

Refer to charts:
2201 ,2202 2218, 2221,
2222, 2223, 2239, 2271, 2289

1

The Heart of the Bay: The Southern Shore

It made sense to begin our search for the ghosts of the Bay along the southeastern shores, for it is here that we hoped to find some of the Bay's oldest ghosts. Centuries ago, Indians and Europeans made their homes along these shores. This area was once the centre of the Bay's activity, whether it was trading, farming, fishing, lumbering, shipping, or just plain homesteading. No matter the occupation, living here was hard work. Ironically, most people come to these shores today to escape work, if only for a week or two.

As we left a small Midland marina on the twenty-six-foot vessel we had called home every July for the last few years, we saw many of these "escapees." Everywhere people were enjoying what the Bay had to offer: her inviting waters, her hypnotic scenery, her wide open spaces and fresh air. We were looking for something else. For below the hustle and bustle of this leisure activity lay another level of energy, a choir of voices with centuries-old stories to tell. We were straining to hear the blend of languages, dialects, and accents that could tell of the hopes, dreams, and adventures of all the people who "broke their backs" to make their mark here. Perhaps the most haunting voices are those of the native men and women who experienced Huronia's turbulent past. Sometimes it's hard to imagine that this peaceful scene, with its sparkling blue water and its lush green islands and shores, is masking a sometimes troubled, passionate, and bloody history.

Midland

Asher Mundy, a very-deaf-former-Quaker-turned-Presbyterian-United-Empire-Loyalist from Kansas held the first town meeting of Tay and Tiny Township at his canteen in 1832. Little did he know "Mundy's Bay" was to become one of the largest and most prosperous cities on the Bay.

The arrival of the railway in the 1870s changed the sleepy village of Mundy's Bay almost overnight. It was renamed Midland (after the railway,) and two large sawmills were built to process the seemingly limitless supply of timber coming down from the northeastern shore and hinterland. The mills could barely keep up and often operated through the night. In one year, the Midland mills sawed more lumber than any of the mills in the prosperous Ottawa Valley.

As trains took out the lumber, they brought in the

people - both settlers and tourists. In 1879, town plans had to be redrawn to include lots for a post office, telegraph office, several hotels, general stores and shops, a saloon, and a boat-building plant. Midland's deep natural harbour attracted freight and passenger vessels and sheltered a fleet of Mackinaw fishing boats. It was boom time and a time of many firsts.

In 1881, the first electric light plant illuminated the mills and yard of the British-American Lumber Company with arc lamps. People from around the Bay made special expeditions by train and steamer to catch their first sight of electricity. About the same time, the company installed a telephone system to link its offices and plants, and the first wooden grain elevator was built on the harbourfront. When Midland incorporated as a town in 1890, its population was an impressive 4,000. It had become one of the most important transshipping ports on the Bay, as well as a centre for lumber and commercial fishing. Not bad for a five-shanty village.

A place as bustling and alive as Midland was not without its sense of humour, according to James Barry in his book, *Georgian Bay, The Sixth Great Lake*. The kind of humour that left a flock of geese, belonging to a Mrs. Deschanes, feeling rather cool. One afternoon the hungry geese fell prey to a few pranksters, who fed them some wheat soaked in whisky. When Mrs. Deschanes returned home she discovered her favourite flock sprawled limply on the ground, and assumed they had been poisoned. Trying to make the most of an unfortunate situation, the resourceful Mrs. Deschanes sat down and plucked them clean. Much to her surprise, they began to sober up and

King Street, Midland, 1890

strut around the yard. She was now the proud owner of a nude flock of geese with a certain fondness for spirits.

No one was exempt from such pranks, not even the town constable. On his wedding night, another trickster poured salt around the constable's house to entice all the village cows to gather for a good "lick." The young new-lyweds were lulled to sleep by the clanking of the cow bells for not one, but two very long nights.

Such practical jokes were only one aspect of the inge-nuity and drive shown by early settlers. In 1883, a young Scot named James Playfair came to Midland to make his fortune in the lumber trade. And indeed, he did, working his way through the mill ranks to take over ownership of one of the original Midland mills, the H.H. Cook Lumber Company. Over the next few years, Playfair expanded his interests to shipping, founding the Midland Navigational Company in 1888 and later the Midland Shipbuilding Company, which produced numerous vessels for the fleets plying the Bay. Playfair was quite a town character, and could often be spotted standing on the balcony of his home, overlooking the harbour, shouting through a megaphone to the captains of ships cruising in and out. In 1926, Playfair's Midland Shipbuilding Company was bought by the Canadian Steamship Company which operated for only a few years before shutting down. During the Second World War it was brought back into operation to build Corvettes, trawlers, and tugs for the British and Canadian Navies. After the war it continued to build bulk freighters but, by 1957, its doors were closed for good.

The Midland City

One of the more notable steamers to come out of the shipyards was the Midland City. Built in 1871, she spent an amazing eighty-four years servicing the Great Lakes. During her last twenty years she became a vital part of the economic and social lives of the cottagers living between Midland and Parry Sound.   In 1921, this 152 -foot (46m) iron side wheeler, the largest ship on the South Channel, began a daily run between Midland and Parry Sound. She would depart at 6 a.m., make numerous stops along the way (the Copperhead Hotel, Go Home Bay and Honey Harbour, to name a few.) She was almost always on time thus earning her the title, "The Heartbeat of Georgian

Bay." Her stops at these many ports were usually big social events for the people who flocked to meet the boat to pick up mail, supplies, or visitors. But people were not the only creatures attracted to the *Midland City*. Huge flocks of gulls regularly trailed behind her, keeping a sharp eye out for scraps thrown overboard by the ship's cook. In fact, the gulls were almost as dependable as the *Midland City* and soon the two became synonymous.

On August 26, 1934, a year after the *Midland City* was converted into a motor vessel, and after more than a half-century of trouble-free service, the ship had her first "wrecking" when she beached six miles (10km) from Midland. As reported by passenger Nora Cooper to the *Toronto Daily Star*, the incident was "a nice Sunday evening shipwreck – with all the thrills and none of the discomforts. There was a lovely sunset on one side," said Miss Cooper, "and just about a full moon on the other. The sun went down shortly after we left the ship, but no one paid much attention to it.... There was just a bump. Nobody thought anything about it. We knew the boat had hit something, but there was nothing to do about it. People looked surprised, but there was not the slightest hint of excitement."

Lifeboats were calmly launched and passenger and crew landed on shore in the near darkness. They lit bonfires and waited for boats from Midland to take them back. "I never saw a crowd take a shipwreck so casually," said Miss Cooper, who returned to Toronto by bus.

The *Midland City* was repaired and ran for another twenty years. But her service was becoming redundant, as more roads were built along the Bay and the car became

The Midland City, "A Nice Quiet Shipwreck"

the transport of choice. And she was feeling her years. Unfortunately, the *Midland City* was not given the send off she deserved after eight decades of labour. On May 7, 1955, she was dismantled, towed to the Wye River, and burned. This was a milestone for the Bay, signaling an end to a vibrant era. For a time, one could dive on the wreck, but the ship has since become part of a break wall located on the easternmost side of the marina at the mouth of the Wye River.

Honeymoon House

Like the break wall created from the Midland City, there is another monument to loss – the loss of love – perched on a hill overlooking Midland's Lakeview Cemetery. Once known as the Haunted Honeymoon House, this two-storey log home was built by Samuel Fraser for his soon-to-be bride, Amelia Jeffery, daughter of a well-known Midland merchant and builder. On the proposed wedding day, June 17, 1858, an elated Samuel Fraser went to his bride's house to inform her and her family of his choice of a minister for the ceremony. Samuel had selected an Anglican minister. The Jefferys were staunchly Presbyterian, not to mention stubborn, and they bluntly objected to his choice. Samuel left their home in a huff, and spent his wedding night with only his own stubbornness and outrage to keep him company. Sadly, Amelia and Samuel never married and spoke to each other again only once, when Samuel apologized for his behavior. Though unlucky in love, Samuel was at least lucky in politics. He became the first Justice of the Peace and Magistrate for Simcoe County and the first Reeve of Tay Township and Midland Village. Both Samuel and Amelia lived in Midland until well into their nineties, but, as this love story would have it, when they died they were buried in separate cemeteries. All that remains of their relationship is the honeymoon home on the hill. It was left empty for many years, allowing Midland children to conjure up all kinds of ghosts, until new owners bought and restored the house in 1944. It is now home to a veterinary clinic.

Even though Midland's sawmills and shipyards have long been silent, the city is still a thriving port, manufacturing centre, and tourist spot. A visit to Midland's Huronia Museum at Little Lake Park is essential to begin understanding the history of the people who shaped the town. The museum displays pioneer, railway, and marine artifacts, and is one of the few places on the Bay that accurately preserves the memory of the area's first inhabitants. A reconstructed seventeenth-century Huron Indian village including longhouses, a shaman's hut, sweat lodges, residences, and canoes, allows you to appreciate and understand the complex and rich cultural lifestyle of these people before they were influenced by Europeans.

Wye Marsh
Sainte-Marie Among the Hurons

The banks of the Wye and these shores have witnessed some extraordinary history. For this was Huronia — a complex community of Huron villages, home to thousands. Here the first European missionaries and settlers lived side-by-side with the Hurons in a handful of small missions scattered throughout the villages. In the beginning, there were many good intentions - one nation earnestly trying to help another by sharing its beliefs, truths, and way of life, and, in the process, learning from the other. For a few years the relationship was harmonious. But as new alliances between Indian groups and Europeans began forming, tension among the tribes escalated. Added to this were power plays, territorial wars, commercial gain, and sadly, an often misguided religious zeal that did more harm than good. The only things that successfully spread were suspicion, disloyalty, hatred, and small pox. It has taken a long time to wash away the blood shed on these shores. Each side, and there are many, strains to tell its truth about what happened. The serenity of the reconstructed Jesuit mission and surrounding village that thrived between 1639 to 1649 can be unnerving as one reflects on the brutal destruction of Huronia and its people.

In the early 1620s, many Jesuit missionaries, including Jean de Brébeuf , came to live among the Huron, bringing to the Indians their Christian religion. At first the Jesuits had a difficult time expressing their beliefs to the Huron and, consequently, were not very successful in the gathering of souls. Many Huron did not trust the Black Robes, as the Jesuit were called. It seemed that wherever they were, so was the strange sickness that was quickly reducing the population of a once strong nation.

Unimpressed by the number of converts, the Superior of the Huron missions, Father Jerome Lalemant, came from France to investigate. Unlike his peer, Jean de Brébeuf, Lalemant had little respect for the people he so desperately wanted to convert. When faced with a rather unfriendly welcome from what he called a "band of demons," he decided to build a mission away from the "intimidating" Huron villages. In exchange for a site three-quarters of a mile (2km) up the Wye River he gave the Huron trinkets, blankets, and other gifts. Construction on the Sainte-Marie mission began. The site quickly developed into an efficient, self-contained village with two churches, a hospital, bakery, blacksmith, carpenter, cookhouse, granary, and an intricate system of canals and locks. Ste. Marie was home to one-fifth of the

European population of New France – sixty-six Europeans of French, Italian, Scottish, or Celtic descent. Some were missionaries, some were donnes (workers who served God but did not take holy orders.) The mission became the focal point of Huronia; central headquarters for the smaller surrounding missions like St. Ignace, St. Louis, and St. Joseph. Lalemant was somewhat satisfied.

But when the age-old feuding between the Hurons and the Iroquois escalated, fueled by territorial disputes and trade wars, Lalemant called for reinforcements. By 1644, Sainte-Marie had soldiers, and its walls and buildings were fortified and insulated. The Iroquois were relentless. From 1647 to 1649, they set Huronia ablaze as they destroyed one Huron village after another. Finally they set upon the missions. Over one thousand Iroquois launched an attack on St. Ignace, about five miles (8km) away from Ste. Marie along the shore. Only three of the mission's four hundred Huron escaped death, or worse, capture, and managed to run through the bush to warn the neighbouring mission of St. Louis, the mission of Jean de Brébeuf. Upon hearing the news, most Huron fled St. Louis, but over eighty Huron and the Jesuits refused to flee. This decision proved costly.

A large Iroquois war party swooped down on the tiny mission, which fought valiantly for almost a full day. But strength in numbers prevailed, and soon most of the Huron were dead or captured. The victorious Iroquois had also captured two Black Robes: Jean de Brébeuf and Lalemant's nephew, Gabriel Lalement. The two were put to death in a most torturous manner, according to donne

Christopher Renault, who helped bring their bodies from St. Ignace to Ste. Marie. The Jesuits were stripped of their flesh, "baptised" with boiling water, their lips cut off to stop them from praying, and finally, their hearts cut out and eaten; an honourable death, according to the Iroquois, one that befit such powerful men.

With St. Ignace taken over by the Iroquois, many Huron deserted the area while others sought temporary refuge at Ste. Marie. Despite regular Iroquois prowlings around its perimeter day and night, the fortified mission was never attacked. However, as if in answer to some silent warning, the surviving Huron and Jesuits left Ste. Marie, burning it to the ground. The small band of about 3,000 Huron and a handful of Jesuits left Huronia to take refuge on Christian Island. (It is rumoured they first stopped on Beausoleil Island to bury what remained of the Jesuit treasure.)

On Christian Island, the Huron and Jesuits built Ste. Marie II and settled in for the winter. Once thought of as sanctuary, it soon became a prison. The island offered little game, and if the Hurons attempted to leave the island to fish or hunt, patrolling Iroquois killed them. With nothing more to eat than acorns, bark, and their dogs, the Huron faced starvation. After a very long winter, only 300 of the original 3,000 survived. Hundreds had died from starvation. One hundred had drowned after falling through the ice while crossing to the mainland to gather food. Some five hundred Huron left the island to join the Iroquois or other tribes. In a last attempt to save their weakened nation the remaining Huron begged the Jesuits to leave the island for New France. The Jesuits agreed.

Hurons at Loretteville, Quebec, 1839

On June 10, 1650, the Jesuits and a few hundred Huron left Christian Island. The once strong Huron nation, and the Jesuits' dream of a new Christian society, had disappeared from the Bay's shores forever.

The Huron people dispersed. Those who moved to New France stayed with the French and established Loretteville, Quebec, where some of their descendants can still be found. A few hundred other Huron joined the Petun scattered between Detroit and northern Ohio. Others joined the Neutrals, while the majority went south to join the Iroquois. The last group began a long journey and are today living in Oklahoma and Kansas. By 1924, there were only 399 Hurons in North America, none of pure lineage. The most powerful nation in the region had been torn apart. A nation had been silenced.

Silenced until the mid-1940s that is, when archaeologists began to research the area. Preliminary excavations began in the 1940s, and by 1954, an archaeological team from the University of Western Ontario led by Dr. William Jury was building a full scale reconstruction of the mission and village. After some three hundred years, Sainte-Marie rose again from her ashes. By 1968, the meticulous reconstruction of the mission on her original site was complete, encapsulating the native and European lifestyles of the time and unfolding the incredible drama that took place on the banks of the Wye. You can walk through the village witnessing a little of the peaceful early seventeenth-century life: tour the medicine lodge, sweat huts, hospital, and churches; listen to the retelling of Huron legend in the long house; grind some corn with the kitchen help; or help the blacksmith with his fire. The award-winning museum offers detailed displays and a film to acquaint people with the mission.

Martyrs' Shrine

Across Highway 12 and up the hill from the mission is the Martyrs' Shrine. Built in 1926, this tall, twin-spired Roman Catholic church honours the eight Jesuit martyrs killed in the Iroquois raids between 1642 and 1649. Canonized by the Pope in 1927, the eight Jesuits were the first saints of North America. This is also the gravesite of Brebeuf and Lalemant.

On the shrine's grounds there is a statue commemorating a ninth martyr, the forgotten martyr, who is only remembered here and in a few historical papers. According to an article written by John Steckley in the *Toronto Star* on September 9, 1978, the forgotten martyr was Joseph Chihwatenha, a Huron who was murdered because of his Christian faith sometime in August 1640. This made him not only the forgotten martyr but the first martyr of the Huronia area.

Joseph was born in 1602 and would have been about thirteen when he saw his first Europeans, Champlain and Le Caron. He was baptised by the Jesuits in 1637, one of the first adult Huron to become a Christian. His conversion was significant because, at the time, almost the only Indians baptised were on their deathbeds. Brébeuf wrote in *The Jesuit Relations* that Joseph was a true son of the Jesuits, refusing to have anything to do with the social and spiritual practices of the Huron. Being a Christian was advantageous for Joseph as he received more money for his furs and more gifts than the other Huron. Nevertheless it is believed he was a sincere convert who zealously promoted Christianity among the Huron and the neighbouring Petun.

In order to entice the Petun to meet with the Jesuits, he encouraged them to trade with the French. This did not sit well with the Huron, who thought Joseph was trying to take the French trade away from them. Not only did they start spreading rumours that Joseph was a traitor, but they also suggested he was a sorcerer, using his new found Christian powers against them — reason enough to plan his murder. Despite the death threats, and the small pox that was wiping out his tribe, Joseph continued to defend the Jesuits and preach their gospel.

In early August, 1640, he left the mission to pick squash and never returned. His body was found in a near-by cornfield, close to present-day Midland. The official word stated he had been killed by a raiding Seneca party. Few believed it. When paying your respect to the eight martyrs in the Martyrs' Shrine, give a nod to the statue of Joseph Chihwatenha. His work was equal to that of the French missionaries. He led many souls into the Jesuit fold, and he died for his beliefs. When remembering Huronia's history, before and after the influences of Europeans, we should remember not only the violence and bloodshed but also the faith, strength, and pride of all the people who lived in and around these palisaded walls.

Wye Marsh Wildlife Centre
Severn Sound Remedial Action Plan

A sanctuary of another kind can be found across Highway 12 at the Wye Marsh Wildlife Centre, which preserves 2,500 acres (1,000ha) of natural marsh habitat. It is open year-round and offers self-guided nature trails, canoe excursions, and cross-country skiing. There is an observation tower overlooking marsh fields and woods, a theatre, numerous indoor exhibits, nature demonstrations, and an underwater viewing room at the edge of the marsh. It is also home to the Severn Sound/Midland Remedial Action Plan (RAP) office. RAPs are multi-level government programs designed to clean up water pollution in forty-three areas of the Great Lakes. Severn Sound is one of the areas of concern, and the Severn Sound RAP's goal is to restore it to health. The main problem is phosphorus pollution, from sources such as sewage treatment plants, agriculture, and runoff. Phosphorus feeds algae, and too much algae makes the water green and murky, unpleasant for swimming and boating. As algae uses up oxygen in the water, it can also harm fish populations. Another concern is the loss of fish and wildlife habitat from development along shorelines and tributaries. Using the ecosystem approach to land-use planning, the Severn Sound RAP is slowly improving water quality and restoring habitat in the watershed. For more information, call 705-526-7809.

Penetanguishene

Toward the end of the War of 1812, Penetanguishene was selected as the site for a southern British naval base because of its excellent sheltered harbour. Military and naval buildings were constructed, and by 1817 men and vessels were sent from Britain. The base was open for business. By 1828, Penetanguishene was the only naval station on the Bay and the only military base on the Upper Great Lakes with over seventy men in its barracks. The joke was, however, that it was also the only military base never to fire a shot.

The War of 1812 had ended soon after construction began on the site, and with the threat of a second American invasion rapidly dwindling, the base became a low priority. What could have been a site of great strategic importance before and during the war was now a skeleton base, manned by minimal staff with few boats. It was

Penetanguishene Naval Establishment, 1832

maintained as a government establishment but suffered budget cuts and overall neglect, eventually closing down in 1856. It was turned over to the Province of Ontario which used the empty buildings as a penal settlement. Then in 1859, it became a reformatory, run by a Captain Moore Kelly. The "boys," some more than twenty years old, were brought by boat and housed in the old officer's barracks until the building of the stone reformatory/prison was completed in 1866. The Boys Reformatory of Upper Canada housed about one hundred inmates and was known for its credible twenty-four-piece brass band. Music wasn't the only activity. Over the years, the reformatory operated a cigar factory, a match factory, a shoe factory, a broom handle factory, a machine shop, and a small laundry - all of which failed.

There was the occasional escape, but "escape to where?" was often the question that ran through an inmate's head when considering it. One boy fled at dusk in a rowboat, only to be found frantically rowing back and forth along the shore by guards the next morning. Exhausted from rowing all night he was an easy catch. It seems he was too scared to beach his boat on shore, thinking the bears might attack him. He was thankful to return to the drudgery.

When the reformatory closed in 1904, it was converted into a hospital for the mentally ill, a precursor to the Ontario Mental Health Centre operating there now. The original reformatory still stands and is being used as the administration office for the Centre.

It is interesting to note that the island in front of the reformatory — Magazine Island — was the storehouse for ammunition belonging to the military base and that it was once connected to the mainland by a bridge.

Although Penetang never reached its full potential as a military site, it did contribute greatly to the area's cultural and historical importance. In 1855, a village sprang up, just south of the base planting Canada's early multicultural seeds with its population of French Canadians, Indians, Métis, British, and other European settlers. As in Midland, a few notable men were responsible for the development of the town. Charles Beck began a small wood delivery service in 1865. Within a decade and a half he was running a mill and manufacturing wood products under the name C. Beck Lumbering Co. Ltd.. There were also two company stores to service his employees (300-400 men) as well as a number of "Beck" homes for rent.

Beck even had his own money coined; the Beck token made of very light metal, was used in a similar way to Beatty's Waubuno notes.

The Beck success story came to an abrupt end one afternoon in 1915 when Charles, now crippled with arthritis, took his daily trip by horse and buggy to the mill yards. He was leading his horse out onto a sand spit to give him water when he turned the buggy too sharply. Beck was thrown into the water and drowned. His sons took over the lumber business, but during the next fifty years, segments of the Beck empire shut down, as the demand for and the supply of lumber fell off.   A number of years ago a freak storm sucked the water out of Penetang Harbour revealing the vestiges of the lumber industry. After hundreds of years the harbour floor was still completely littered with sawdust and sunken logs.

Penetanguishene's historical importance as the only military station on the Bay convinced Ontario's Ministry of Tourism to restore and rebuild the Historic Naval and Military Establishments, known as Discovery Harbour. Today the tall sails of the schooners the *Bee*, the *Perseverance,* and the *Tecumseh* welcome you to a living historical community, complete with naval and military demonstrations, at the north end of Penetang's inner harbour. The full-scale schooner replicas are moored at the historic wharf, while the museum, within walking distance of the public dock, offers a glimpse of Penetang as an early lumber town.

Present Island

The settlement at Penetanguishene marked the beginning of a great wave of European immigration to the shores of Georgian Bay. Over the next hundred years, thousands of people came to seek their fortune and they all needed land on which to settle. At the time Georgian Bay Indians were living on most of the prime farming land. The British government struck a deal with them. In exchange for the rights to the Indian land, the British government distributed annual payments at set locations around the Bay. Present Island was among the first of these locations.

Since the first treaty was signed in 1798, more than

Present Giving, moved to Manitoulin Island in 1836

2,000 Georgian Bay Indians had gathered here to receive allotments of cloth, linen, blankets, thread, knives, tobacco, flags, flints, guns, kettles, and other trinkets. Although these goods were actually payments, the Indians saw them as presents, hence the island's name.

Present-giving ceremonies were also held at Amherstburg, Lake Simcoe, Drummond Island and Penetanguishene. In 1836, the ceremony was moved to Manitoulin island in an effort to encourage the Indians to leave the southern shores altogether and move north, where the British governement felt they could be better managed. The natives complied. More and more were losing their lands, signing treaties they didn't fully understand. Some fought back (p. 207), while some resigned themselves to life on the reserve. The formal transfer of gifts eventually stopped, but the legacy of land rights transactions and disputes continues today.

The Wawinet Wreck

On the dark and dreary night of September 21, 1942, a group of exhausted, drenched men, some still wearing their overcoats, pulled themselves up on the shore of Beausoleil Island. They were the lucky ones, the survivors of perhaps one of the most tragic and mysterious shipwrecks in the area - the *Wawinet*.

The excursion on the *Wawinet* began innocently enough as a company outing. The yacht's owner, Bert Corbeau, a onetime professional hockey player who played with the Montreal Canadiens, took his fellow employees from the Midland Foundry & Machine

Hockey player Bert Corbeau lost his life on theWawinet

Company and a few visitors on a leisurely fishing trip. There were forty-one people on board the seventy-nine-foot (24m) yacht. On their return to Penetang from Honey Harbour, the overcrowded *Wawinet* made a sudden turn, listing until the open lower windows were underwater. Within two minutes she filled and sank. A group of survivors, mostly those on deck, were able to swim a quarter of a mile (.4km) to the shore of Beausoleil Island, their way lit by the moon. Those who couldn't swim floated on the few available life preservers until other swimmers took turns helping them to shore. The survivors were picked up from Beausoleil and taken to

Midland, where the news of the tragedy spread quickly. Another survivor was retrieved from Present Island. Most of the passengers, including Corbeau, were not as fortunate.

The wreck itself is an eerie reminder of that September night. As if it is reluctant to tell its sad tale it can be difficult to find. The sinking took place off Beausoleil Point. On the chart, draw a line from the red marker located east off Present Island to the narrow hook point west of Beausoleil Point. Along this line search between the land and the black marker. A fish finder may be needed to locate it in about 20 to 25 feet (6 to 7.5m) of murky water. Visibility is very low – less than two feet (.6m). Finding this wreck requires patience and perseverance. It took us six hours, two boats, and a fish finder to eventually locate the *Wawinet*. But it was worth it. When you do find it, use a light and a rope to guide yourself to and from the site. The *Wawinet* is sitting upright and intact except for her stern and deck. It is also a fantastic site to see fish. *NOTE: The low visibility and heavy boating traffic are hazardous.*

Beausoleil Island
Georgian Bay Islands National Park

Like the Bay (p.xiii), Beausoleil Island has been called many names by many people. The Indians called it Pamidonegog, which seems a mouthful until you compare it to the English translation: "an island in the centre of a

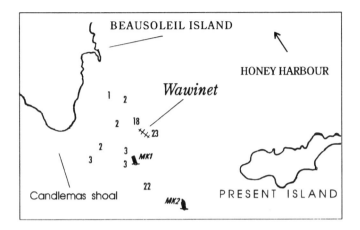

Refer to chart 2202, sheet 1

big channel, a shelter and protection from the open sea."
French traders called it St. Ignace, and it was also known
for a time as Prince William Harry Island, after a brother
of George III. Finally, in 1819, a French Canadian settled
here, naming the island after himself: Beausoleil, meaning
beautiful sun. An apt name, as Beausoleil is one of the
best places on the Bay to watch the sun set.

    There are many stories about Beausoleil, the oldest
and perhaps the most tragically romantic being that of
Wahsoona and the silver birch. While the heartbroken
Huron god Kitchikewana was having his temper tantrum,
digging into the ground and throwing dirt in the water,
many heavy rocks fell from his hands. Some of these rocks
accidentally killed Wahsoona, the popular daughter of
one of the Indian chiefs. Everyone grieved her death, and

in commemoration of her, another god, Kijemahuedoo, ordained silver birch to grow forever on the island.

The birch trees also stand guard over an ancient Indian burial ground located near the park office and fire tower. It is the final resting place of many of the old warrior chiefs, who now enjoy the beautiful sunsets for eternity.

There might be more than old bones buried on Beausoleil. Before the Jesuits and Hurons fled to Christian Island to seek refuge from the Iroquois, it was said they stopped on Beausoleil to bury what remained of the Jesuit treasure. Somewhere by Treasure Bay on the northeast side of the island, there is supposed to be a two-foot long stone with a Latin inscription that marks the place where a pot of French and Spanish silver coins and a collection of guns and other relics from the Jesuit mission were buried. It has yet to be uncovered.

The island, once a prehistoric hunting and fishing ground and, more recently, an Ojibwa Indian reserve, is now part of the Georgian Bay Islands National Park. Beausoleil is the largest of the 59 islands in the park and serves as its hub. Five miles (8 km) in length and one and a quarter miles (2 km) wide, it is a heavily wooded game sanctuary open to campers, hikers, and picnickers. The park includes 15 campgrounds with 200 sites; 13 of the campgrounds are on Beausoleil. There are docks at Cedar Spring and Ojibwa Bay, as well as a public wharf for day-use only, on the island's eastern shore. The island is home to the endangered Eastern Massasauga rattlesnake. If you spot one, kindly give it the right of way. There are also a few wrecks around Beausoleil which may be of interest.

Indian Belle Wreck

There is an old tradition on the Bay of naming a rock after the ship that founders on it and so an unknown wreck, just off Indian Belle Rock, is often referred to as the Indian Belle wreck.

This three-masted sailing ship is located between Beausoleil Island and Giant's Tomb, near Fraser Bank. Enter the water 100 yards (90m) west of the two rocks exposed on the southernmost part of Fraser Bank. The 130-foot (39m) wreck lies in less than 15 feet (4.5m) of water. Her wooden hull pieces, with steel spikes jutting out, lie flat on the bottom. Plenty of small mouth bass and other marine life keep you company as you swim about the wreck. It is an excellent site for snorkeling or for the novice diver. *NOTE: Be cautious of the shoals in the area and any strong west or north wind. There can also be a strong current.*

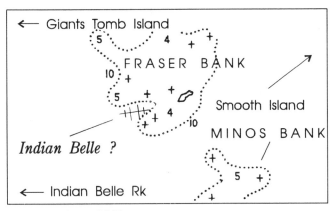

Refer to chart 2239

The Luckport and Reliever Wrecks

After fifty-four years of service, the *Luckport*'s luck ran out one day in December 1934, when she caught fire and sank west of Sawlog Point. Her charred hull is all that can be found at the site, about 200 feet (60m) from shore in 12 to 25 feet (3.6-7.5m) of water. And, even though on sunny days she's visible from the surface, a lot of luck, plenty of search time, and a good map are needed to find what is left of this wooden steamer. There are no prominent landmarks near the site and you must dive from a boat to access this site as the nearby beach is privately owned.

The *Reliever* suffered a similar fate to the *Luckport*. On November 3, 1906, this large steamer tug caught fire while taking on a load of lumber at a sawmill on the mainland. In order to save the mill and the dock, she was cut afloat, eventually running aground on Ways Point at the west side of Methodist Bay and burning to the waterline. Although the fire claimed no lives, the wreck caused a later tragedy, as Bill Northcott tells in his impressive history of this area, *Thunder Bay Beach*. In 1921, Robert Leroux and his family were having a picnic at Methodist Point. Robert went for a walk to inspect the *Reliever*. While on the wreck, he lost his footing and fell into a hole. Trapped beneath the wreck, he drowned. His family was unable to recover his body until the next day.

All that is left of the *Reliever*, a few boards from her hull and other remains scattered along the sandy bottom, is located in up to 12 feet (3.6m) of water, about 100 feet (30m) off Ways Point. You can access this wreck by boat or from the shore of Awenda Provincial Park.

Luckport, Lucknow & Fanny at Midland Harbour

Giants Tomb Island
Awenda Provincial Park

Giants Tomb represents more than 11,000 years of Native history and legend, beginning with how it acquired its name. The great Huron god Kitchikewana lived on the shores of Georgian Bay, protecting all her inhabitants. He was a god of immense size, who wore a headdress made from the feathers of a thousand birds and a grand necklace of tree stumps over his six-hundred-beaver pelt robe. Kitchikewana's emotions matched, if not surpassed, his enormous physical proportions. He had a temper and was prone to fits of anger, restlessness, and agitation. The Hurons figured he needed a woman to calm him down, so they selected some of their more beautiful, even-tempered young girls and displayed them for the god. Kitchikewana chose the lovely Wanakita for his bride. But she had plans of her own, and rejected the god to marry a warrior from her own tribe. The grief-stricken Kitchikewana flew into a rage, scooping up huge handfuls of earth and throwing them into the Bay. Heartbroken and exhausted, he lay down at the base of the islands and went to sleep forever, his form creating Giants Tomb's silhouette. His temper tantrum was also said to be responsible for the creation of one of Georgian Bay's more popular cottage areas. The five bays around the southern shore are said to be formed by the gouging action of Kitchikewana's powerful fingers, and the handfuls of dirt that Kitchikewana violently threw into the water became the 30,000 Islands.

The sad resting spot of the great Kitchikewana is now part of the Awenda Provincial Park and is a popular spot for picnics, swimming, fishing, and camping, with 200 private, sheltered sites for overnight use. The mainland area of the park also offers campsites and hiking trails along beautiful stone beaches, boulder fields, kettle lakes, sand dunes, and bluffs. The Park protects over 4,838 acres (1,935 ha) of Ontario's most significant geological and historical features, including six nature reserve zones. There is also an interesting dive and snorkeling site highlighting the unique geological features found along the southeastern shore of Giants Tomb Island.

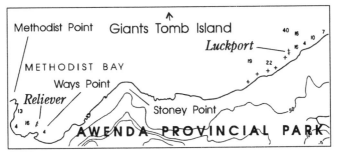

Refer to chart 2239

Beckwith Island

Bill Northcott tells a story about Beckwith Island in *Thunder Bay Beach* that is a reminder of the Bay's indiscriminate power. On September 4, 1924 Arthur Visick, his wife and two children, aged five and seven, set out for an afternoon picnic and cruise around Christian and Beckwith Islands. After a few hours, they noticed the weather was turning for the worst so they headed for home. As the Visicks reached the southeast tip of Beckwith Island, the boat battery died. They rowed to shore, anchored the boat, and set about making a shelter to wait out the storm. In the morning, not only were they greeted by the continuing storm but the relentless winds had swept away their boat. They were stranded. Arthur set out to see if they were alone. He discovered the remains of two lumber camps and a bit of lunch - a dried-up stash of food. This, plus the remainder of their picnic and some blackberries, was all they had to eat. The storm continued to blow forcing the Visicks to spent three miserable days on the island until a concerned neighbour initiated their rescue.

Beckwith Island is now an Indian Reserve. Its cove serves as a good shelter from the strong southwest winds.

NOTE: Make sure you are anchored securely.

The Thomas Cranage Wreck

This wreck has the dubious distinction of being the largest wooden vessel ever lost on the Bay. On September 25, 1911, the 305-foot (92m) *Thomas Cranage* was on her way from Detroit to the Tiffin elevator on the east side of Midland when she ran aground on Watcher's Reef, north-

Thomas Cranage, largest wooden vessel lost on the Bay

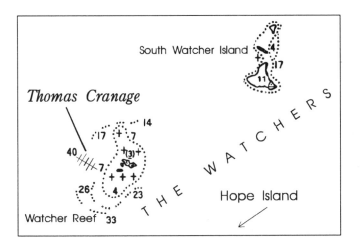

South Watcher Island

Thomas Cranage

THE WATCHERS

Hope Island

Watcher Reef

Refer to chart 2239

east of Giant's Tomb. The cargo and seventeen-member crew were saved, but the *Thomas Cranage* was so firmly aground on the reef she had to be left to the mercy of the ruthless autumn storms.

The site can easily be seen from the surface and is sometimes marked by a white milk jug. Her bottom and engine are on Watcher's Reef, while her rudder and other debris are scattered across the east side of the reef in 15 to 25 feet (4.5 to 7.5m) of water.

A wreck of this size is humbling. As you swim above her and see her huge timbers scattered over the reef, the power and magnitude of a Bay storm becomes very clear.

NOTE: Be cautious of the reef in rough weather. The openness of the site makes it vulnerable to adverse westerly weather. Tie your boat securely while exploring the wreck. The Collingwood Bulletin of November 16, 1911, tells of Paul Desone and Charles Martin from Penetang who were stranded on the reef for four days without food or shelter when their boat broke away from its mooring as they explored the wreck.

Hope Island
Hope Island Lighthouse

The natives used to call this island Giant's Island because they could hear a giant's footsteps and feel the ground shake under his weight. As this island was obviously occupied by the gods, Hurons would not come here. It has also been suggested that this is why the Hurons and Jesuits took refuge on Christian Island instead of Giant's Island.

The Hope Island Lighthouse was built in 1884 on the island's northeast tip. It features a square tower, 57 feet (17m) in height from the ground to the lantern and its light is visible from 12 miles in all directions. Trouble began on the island in 1891, when light keeper Allan Collins traded postings with Christian Island lightkeeper John Hoare, so Collins' children could attend the school on Christian Island. A great deal of quarreling erupted over trade, a sailboat, a stove, and other important matters. The Superintendent of Lighthouses was forced to settle the dispute. He sided with Collins. Hoare, to say the least, was not pleased.

Shortly thereafter, Hoare was replaced by a fellow

Hope Island Lighthouse

named Thomas Marchildon. While working in his garden one day, Marchildon narrowly missed being hit by a bullet that went whizzing by his head - a bullet from John Hoare's gun. This was nothing new. Ever since he first set foot on the island, Hoare had given him a "shot-gun welcome." Marchildon spent his first few weeks after his arrival camping just a little out of gunshot range of the lighthouse, until the ice became solid enough to cross to the mainland for reinforcements.

Marchildon might not have been Hoare's only target. According to local legend, two fishermen were reported murdered and buried in the well under the lighthouse. No bodies were found but rumour persisted that their graves

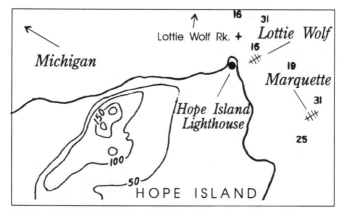

Refer to chart 2239

were somewhere on the island. Many longtime residents say that on his deathbed, John Hoare confessed to the murders. Supposedly the two fishermen had rescued Hoare from a suicide attempt, a rescue that Hoare did not want and for which he may have taken revenge.

The Hope Island Lighthouse now operates automatically - it's safer that way - and is designated an historic building. The island, like Beckwith and Christian Islands, is also an Indian reserve.

The Marquette Wreck

The captain of the *Marquette* had no other choice. The 139-foot (42m) schooner had seen many storms in her decade of service on the Lakes, but none as fierce as the one on November 20, 1867. She was crossing the Bay on her way to Penetang when a blinding snowstorm hit, and the Captain had to beach her at Hope Island. Even then, the high, rolling waves flooded her with bone chilling water. Her crew pumped desperately, giving up only when the water poured over her gunwales. They finally abandoned ship to seek shelter on the island. For two days and nights, they helplessly watched the relentless November waves pound the *Marquette*.

The *Marquette* is probably the best wreck in the area. A classic. Located just off the northeast shore of Hope Island, she is very easy to find as a tire float marks her location. Search for her halfway between the lighthouse and the first point off Hope Island, about a half-mile (.8 km) from shore. As we descended the rope of the tire float, we saw nothing but black water, until, in about 40 feet (12m) of water, the *Marquette* silently appeared, resting peacefully on the sandy bottom. Her mighty anchors stretched out from the bow; the exact place where over a hundred years earlier a frantic crew had let them out in a last attempt to save her.

Discovered in 1975, the relatively intact wreck still sits upright. Her deck is gone but the bow and sides of the hull remain. Her windlass, capstan, and centreboard lie in the sand-filled interior. There are also several nautical artifacts to see, making it an excellent site for photographers. The *Marquette* wreck served as a training dive for a group of disabled divers who spent many hours and many dives cleaning and restoring the wreck, making it the dramatic and powerful dive it is today.

The Lottie Wolf, foundered 1879

The Lottie Wolf Wreck

As the evening sun set, we could see from the flying bridge of our boat the *Lottie Wolf's* long dark silhouette in the light blue water. It was a calm clear evening, quite unlike the stormy night some 110 years ago.

Bound for Midland with a cargo of corn in 1879, the 126-foot (37 m), three-masted schooner was making her way through heavy weather when she hit a rock (thereafter named Lottie Wolf Rock) off the northeast shore of Hope Island. She began to fill rapidly as the captain purposely ran her into the sand in front of the lighthouse. Like the *Marquette's* crew, the crew of the *Lottie Wolf* had to abandon ship and watch the storm break up their schooner.

The main body of the wreck is settled on the sandy bottom about 150 yards (135m) from the lighthouse dock, directly in line with the painted red vertical line where the lighthouse tower joins the housing. In front of the lighthouse, in about, 18 feet (5.4m) of water, lie three sections of the ship. Approximately 50 feet (15m) to the left (when facing the lighthouse,) there are steel pieces, gears, and other debris scattered in the sand.

The Michigan Wreck

The 297-foot (89.1m) steel barge became another casualty of the Bay's winds and waves when she was driven ashore off Hardhead Point on the northwest corner of Hope Island. On November 24, 1943, the *Michigan* was removing grain cargo from another ship, the *Riverton*, off Hope Island, when she was blown into the shallows by strong winds. The *Riverton* managed to escape unharmed along with the *Michigan*'s crew. But the barge wasn't so lucky as she broke up on the shoal and sank in 5 to 15 feet (1.5 to 4.5m) of water.

The wreck is located near a particular cluster of rocks - one large boulder with numerous small ones set around it, and is marked by a white milk bottle. This is a fascinating site for both diver and snorkeler as there is plenty of machinery, metal works, huge cogs, half portholes, and other nautical artifacts scattered over the shoal. *NOTE: shoals and the strong westerly winds can be a dangerous combination.*

The Michigan, which wrecked on Hope Island, 1943

Christian Island/ Ste. Marie II
Christian Island Lighthouse

Sainte Marie II on Christian Island was the last home of the remaining 3,000 Hurons from the great nation which once populated the southeastern shores of Georgian Bay. Along with about sixty Frenchmen and a dozen Jesuits, the starving and sick Hurons spent one long winter on this island, living at Fort Ste. Marie II before abandoning Georgian Bay for New France (p12). Unlike the other missions, Ste. Marie II was constructed of stone, not fortified with wooden palisades, and was lived in for only one year. When the Huron left the Bay on June 10, 1650, Fort Ste. Marie II was abandoned. It has since crumbled

Christian Island Lighthouse, 1880

after centuries of exposure to the Bay's harsh elements.

As early as 1965, several excavations by independent archaeologists and the University of Toronto's Department of Anthropology have uncovered numerous French and Huron artifacts: a 1640 coin, a gun flint, pieces of copper, beads, and pottery. Since 1987, the Beausoleil First Nation — who are spread out over Beckwith and Hope Islands as well as Christian Island — and the London Museum of Archaeology have been excavating this site, uncovering evidence of the European living quarters, just north of the fort. Visitors to Christian Island, can view the excavation sites of Fort Ste. Marie II including the stone walls encasing the fort, the Huron village, and the European compound.

Also of historical interest is Christian Island's lighthouse, the first to be built on Georgian Bay. Completed in 1854, the 60-foot (18m) stone lighthouse and stone residence were located on Bar Point on the southern tip of the island. William Hoare was appointed its first keeper after his discharge from the Royal Navy. In 1868, his infamous son John took over as the youngest Bay lighthouse keeper at the tender age of twenty-two (see p.34 for details of his strange career!) This lighthouse, like Hope Island's, has been automated and declared an historic building. The ruins of the old stone house that once stood proudly next to the lighthouse are still there with half the back wall and fireplace intact. Tiger lilies and long grass make a natural carpet inside the house. Watch for poison ivy.

The Saucy Jim Wreck

For just over two decades, the *Saucy Jim* was busy plying the Bay, towing, wrecking, freighting - whatever would pay. Her multipurpose career was cut short when she caught fire while moored at Christian Island on November 18, 1910. The little steamer tug was a total loss.

Today her boiler can be seen sticking up out of about five feet (1.5m) of water along a sandy beach just north of the ferrydock on Christian Island. Because the wreck is in such shallow water, it is perfect for snorkeling and swimming around.

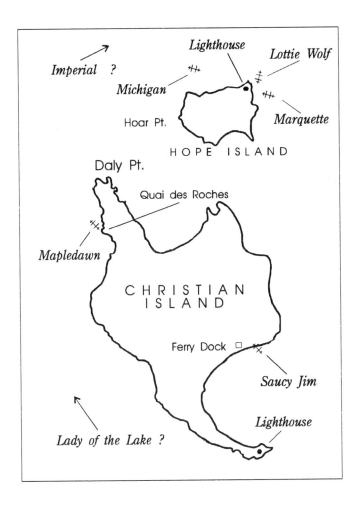

Refer to charts 2201, 2239, 2289

The Mapledawn

The Mapledawn Wreck

The *Mapledawn* was yet another victim of the Bay's notorious November gales. On November 30, 1924, the 350-foot (105m) steel lake freighter was on its way to Midland with a cargo of grain when a heavy snowstorm hit. She strayed off course and was wrecked off the Quai des Roches on the northwest corner of Christian Island. A good portion of her cargo was recovered, and some machinery was moved but the freighter was a total loss. During World War II, some of the wreck was raised for metal salvage. As a result of the tearing up of the vessel, there are some interesting underwater landscapes of massive, twisted metal to explore on this, the largest wreck on the Bay. The main sections of the vessel, where the winch, chains, engine, and gigantic boilers can be found are 20 to 30 feet (6 to 9m) down. The propeller lies in 30 feet (9m) of water, approximately 50 feet (15m) off her stern. Snorkeling over the site is also possible on clear, sunny days. The Mapledawn wreck is located about 100 yards (90m) from shore, off the east side of Daly Point on the northwest side of Christian Island. It can be seen from the surface. Consult the chart for exact location.

Nottawasaga Bay
The Nancy Island Historic Site

The Nancy was a private cargo vessel brought into service by the British as a supply ship. She played a key role in the War of 1812. Not only did she transport much needed supplies, but her fiery demise provided the motivation to capture two key American ships, which eventually hastened the end of the war and the signing of the Treaty of Ghent in 1814.

In September 1813, during the Battle of Put-In-Bay on Lake Erie, the established British supply route to the Upper Great Lakes fell under American control. Now it was very difficult for the British to transport goods to the garrison at Fort Mackinac (between Lakes Huron and Michigan.) As an alternative, the British began using a "back door" route, bringing supplies up the Nottawasaga River to the *Nancy*, which then transported them to Fort Mackinac.

American schooners began to patrol in search of the

The Nancy played a key role in theWar of 1812

Nancy, determined to capture her and starve out the British. The British kept a step ahead of the Americans by sending a scout from Fort Mackinac to alert the *Nancy's* crew. Her lieutenant, Miller Worsley, heeded the warning, turned the ship around, and hid her about two miles up the Nottawasaga River. The crew hastily built a boathouse in which to store her cargo. However, on August 14, 1814, the masts of the American ships the *Niagara, Scorpion* and *Tigress* were spotted. The Americans opened fire, hitting the boathouse which burst into flames. Fire spread to the *Nancy* and she burned to the waterline and sank. Her crew, once again blessed with foresight, had earlier loaded all supplies into canoes and

The Nancy's charred hull may have formed an obstruction in the river causing silt buildup to form Nancy Island.

bateaux and hidden them upstream. Once the Americans had left the area, the *Nancy's* crew cautiously made the six-day journey to the Fort. All was not a loss but Lieutenant Worsley still wanted revenge.

He and a small crew set out to find the American ships that had destroyed their beloved "workhorse." They spotted the *Tigress* sitting smugly alone on the Bay, secure in the belief that the Americans had gained control of all the transport routes along the Upper Great Lakes. The *Nancy* crew quite easily snuck up and overtook her crew. Worsley left the American flag flying, and dressed his men in the Americans' uniforms. When the unsuspecting

Scorpion approached the *Tigress* she was almost effortlessly captured by Worsley's men. The ships, now under British command, were renamed *Confiance* and *Surprise,* and the *Nancy's* name regained its glory. The British regained control of transport routes thus hastening the end of the war. They had learned their lesson. Their military and naval establishments were moved from Fort Mackinac to Penetanguishene (see p.17).

The *Nancy* lay in the mud for 114 years, until her hull was recovered in 1928. It is now located inside the Museum of the Upper Lakes on Nancy Island near Wasaga Beach.

Although the Nottawasaga River and Bay were ineffective as a reliable harbour, the rivermouth was considered an excellent location for the Bay's first railway depot... until yet another nautical tragedy tainted its shores. The site was black-marked as a transshipping port when the two-masted schooner *H.B. Bishop* ran firmly aground during a storm. She was originally anchored offshore loading grain from smaller scows when a wind hit her broadside and ran her up on land. Her crew was able to step safely off the ship, but she was a total loss. The railway terminus went to Collingwood instead.

It would be another form of transportation, the automobile, that would bring notoriety to Nottawasaga Bay. Her magnificent stretch of beaches attracted vacationers as early as the 1900s, and they keep on coming every year. Numerous summer cottages, resorts, motels, restaurants, and amusement parks now blanket the beaches of this once "useless" stretch of shore.

Wasaga Beach when you could park on the beach

Wasaga Beach

There are 11 beaches in the area, of which Wasaga Beach is the largest and most active. The "busy-ness" of its petting zoos, amusement parks, minigolf and go-kart courses, water parks, summer resorts, motels, ferris wheels, bowling alleys and bingo games hum with the same liveliness as did the Indian fishing villages, the British naval establishment and the lumbering communities dotting its shores years ago when the area was known as Schooner Town. One might think with all these distractions the past would get lost here, but it hasn't. The Nancy Island Historic Site, the Museum of the Upper Lakes and the Schooner Town

Parkette provide vivid and dramatic reminders of the defeats and triumphs experienced while shaping this part of our nation. Wasaga Beach was the site of an airstrip for the first flight from mainland Canada to England which took place in 1934. James Ayling and Leonard Reid were the pilots. A plaque commemorating the event was erected on Nancy Island. There is also a provincial park offering 9 miles (14km) of clean, sandy beaches for those looking to get away from the neon strip of commercialism - the "Coney Island" of the North.

Collingwood
Collingwood Shipyards

Once called Hen and Chickens, due to the shape and layout of a nearby set of islands, the town was christened Collingwood over a bottle of wine by three directors of the Toronto and Lake Simcoe Railway and the town sheriff. A railway terminus was being built which was going to make the place a boom town, and a boom town called Hen and Chickens just did not seem appropriate. There was another thing. Collingwood's shallow harbour meant that ships had to unload onto a boulder located where the dry dock now stands. In 1858, in line with their increasingly sophisticated image, J.H. Smith built a wharf which extended out from the head of Hurontario Street.

The town was incorporated in 1858, the same year William Watts came to town and began building the most popular small vessel on the Bay... his "Collingwood skiff." It was between 20 and 35 feet long, double-ended, and powered by one or two sails. With the centreboard up, it was shallow of draft - a necessity in Georgian Bay waters - and when the centreboard was down, it was capable of managing most of Georgian Bay's weather conditions. It met the needs of pleasure boaters and fishermen alike.

Dry Dock at the Collingwood Shipyard

Watts' design was copied all across the Great Lakes where his utilitarian vessel eventually became known as the Mackinaw. On the larger end of the scale, the Collingwood Shipyards produced tankers, bulk carriers, naval vessels, freighters, and passenger carriers. Between 1947 and 1980, it constructed over 100 steel ships, ferries and barges.

Boatbuilder William Watts

The two local passenger lines running out of Collingwood competed fiercely. The Great Northern Transit Company — or White Line because all their vessels were white — and The North Shore Navigation Company — or Black Line because their vessels were black — used to race each other from port to port. For $10, one could go on a five-day return cruise including meals from Collingwood to Owen Sound to Sault Ste. Marie to Mackinac or take daily departures to Manitoulin and the Sault. In 1899 the Black Line bought out the White Line, forming the Northern Navigation Company centered in Sarnia, Ontario. A few years later, it became part of Canada Steamship Lines. As the popularity of the auto-

The Ploughboy almost foundered July 1859 with noted passenger Sir John A. Macdonald (see page 290)

mobile grew, the need for passenger lines decreased, leaving only one on the Bay's waters today - the *Chi-Cheemaun*, which runs between Tobermory and South Baymouth from the end of April to mid-October.

Collingwood was the proud home port of such vessels as the *Northern Belle,* the *Atlantic*, the *Baltic,* and the fastest of them all, the *Pacific*. Great seafaring captains such as Black Pete Campbell, so named for his black hair and sideburns, also hailed from here. One of the premier skippers on the Lakes, people said he had "the luck of the devil."

It was fortunate that he was lucky, for Collingwood

was far from a tragedy-free port. Two of the most mysterious and still talked-about shipping disasters were linked to this harbour. On November 21, 1879, the *Waubuno* fatefully left in the wee hours of the morning after it had earlier delayed its departure for Parry Sound due to stormy weather, and the *Asia* first embarked from Collingwood before heading to Owen Sound on September 13, 1882, only to go to her watery grave.

Whispers and accusations of murder have also tainted Collingwood harbour. In July 1863, the *Ploughboy* was returning to Collingwood from Manitoulin Island when William Gibbard, an official of the Crown Land Department, failed to appear for breakfast. A crew member went to rouse him from his bed but he was not there. He was no where to be found. Gibbard had been sent to Manitoulin to settle a dispute between the Jesuits and natives and the island's few settlers. The Jesuits and natives wanted an independent government and wanted the settlers removed from their land. They went so far as to try to forcibly remove the settlers themselves. At this point Gibbard and the police interfered to quell the uprising. After his disappearance, a few government men returned to Manitoulin to look for him. They found his body floating near Little Current, a deep gash on his forehead.

One theory about his death is that an Indian was sent by the Jesuits to kill Gibbard on board the *Ploughboy* or before boarding, in retaliation for his interference with their land claims. The other theory suggests Gibbard boarded the *Ploughboy* and was killed by one of the crew members, then robbed, as it was common knowledge he was carrying $2,000 in treaty payments. The $2,000 was found in the ship's safe, but Gibbard's wallet was later found missing, as were the ship's porter and bartender when the *Ploughboy* docked at Collingwood. The mystery remains.

Collingwood offers many attractions for today's explorer of the past. The Collingwood Shipyards are closed, but are still accessible by water if you are interested in surveying the area from your boat. (permission is needed to dock or to go ashore.) The land is private property but you can bring your boat in to the former dry docks (now full of water) to view the giant warehouses of early nineteenth-century Collingwood. The city is presently debating whether to zone the area for a commercial harbour and park (and build a new marina) or to zone it for retail and residential use and build condominiums.

The harbour is also one of the forty-three areas in the Great Lakes developing and implementing Remedial Action Plans (RAPs). The RAP involves community members in environmental rehabilitation programs designed to restore a healthy aquatic environment for the benefit of all living things. Since 1988, the community has worked towards cleaning up Collingwood's industrial past, rehabilitating lost habitat, and promoting pollution prevention with the long-term goal of transforming the Town and Collingwood Harbour into a vibrant ecosystem. The office is located at 275 First Street.

The Collingwood Museum, residing in a former railroad station across the street from the shipyards, offers an excellent chronicle of Collingwood's earliest inhabitants, the Petun Indians of Nottawasaga, and of the town's later developments in shipping, railroads, and fishing. It also offers a walking tour of historic Collingwood.

The Mary Ward Wreck

Alcohol, defective instruments, misleading or "haunted" lights, fate... one or all of these could have caused the sinking of the *Mary Ward*. And, with chilling hindsight, patience would have saved a few of the passengers.

The *Mary Ward* was a 120-foot (36m) steamer that left Sarnia for Collingwood in November 1872, full of salt, coal oil and a number of passengers. After picking up more passengers at Tobermory and then Owen Sound on the morning of November 24th, she set off for Collingwood. It was a pleasant Sunday to be on the Bay but as it was late Fall the night dropped fast and visibility became a problem. The captain was having trouble with the compass and could not pick up the Nottawasaga lighthouse. Finally, he spotted a light and adjusted his course. Unfortunately, it was not the light from the lighthouse but from the Craigleith Boarding House located between Collingwood and Owen Sound. Before the captain could correct the error, the steamer ran aground on the smooth shelf-like shoal of Milligan's Reef about three miles (5 km) from shore. The boat was in no immediate danger, so two men were sent out in a lifeboat at about 9 p.m. to get a tug from Collingwood. They arrived in Collingwood early Monday morning and arranged for the *Mary Ann* to retrieve the *Mary Ward*.

Back at the *Mary Ward*, the weather was turning stormy so the captain and seven others left in another lifeboat to get help at the lighthouse. As the storm brewed, the lifeboat began to take in water, and they barely made it to shore. The mighty waves and wind prevented the *Mary Ann* from reaching the *Mary Ward*. As she turned back to Collingwood her crew stared in horror at the shrieking passengers they were leaving behind. Panic had set in on the *Mary Ward*. Weighing their odds at 50-50, eight men decided to row ashore. But this time, the Bay proved too powerful. The waves swept the men away two-by-two, spinning the boat and plucking off its desperate victims. A huge crest swept over the boat, dumping the remaining two men in the water where they clung desperately to the gunnels. As the cold numbed their grip, they slowly let go and drowned with the six others.

The storm eventually passed and three Collingwood fishing boats rescued the remaining cold and shaken passengers. Some survivors claim that the captain had been drinking. Others suggest that he was using an improper logging device of his own design instead of the one on the ship. Whatever the cause, the loss of the eight men was felt throughout the Bay. Legend has it that their souls haunted the Craigleith Boarding House for years in revenge for sending the *Mary Ward* off course. The spirits were finally laid to rest when the Boarding House was torn down.

The *Mary Ward's* cargo and most of her hardware were eventually salvaged. But the Bay had not yet finished with the steamer. Over the years, she continued to beat away at the ship, sinking her farther into the depths. The

The Mary Ward gave her name to a shoal in November 1872.

reef was renamed the Mary Ward Shoal. A commemorative plaque honouring the memory of the victims and the brave rescuers is located at Craigleith Provincial Park.

The wreck can be found about two miles (9.6m) from shore, just beyond the second shoal north of Thornbury and Collingwood. She is near the second buoy (marked with a TN6) from the north of the lighthouse. Go straight towards the notch in the mountain. The main part of the wreck lies in less than 20 feet (6m) of water, inside the second reef from the open water to the north. The site is very difficult to locate. We couldn't find it on our last trip. It's best to go on a good day when the visibility is high. When you do find the wreck, it is about 90 to 100 feet (27 to 30m) in length and contains a five-foot (1.5m) driveshaft, a three-blade propeller, engine parts, and the keel complete with protruding ribs.

NOTE: *Be wary of the shoal — we don't want to be writing about you in our next edition.*

The Nottawasaga Light

For those who remained on the *Mary Ward*, Nottawasaga lightkeeper Captain George Collins and his assistant and son, Charles, were a welcome sight. Along with the help of three fishing boats from Collingwood, the lightkeepers rescued twenty-four frightened people from the stranded steamer. For their efforts, besides the hugs and handshakes, each received $15 from the Canadian government. But it was nothing out of the ordinary for the island's first two keepers of the light. During their careers George (1858-1890) and Charles (1859-1872) were credited with saving fifty-two people. (Sadly, Charles was unable to save his own life a few years later when he drowned while fishing, near the Mary Ward Shoal.)

George Collins was the first keeper of this eighty-six foot (25.8m) lighthouse, one of six Imperial Towers built on Lake Huron and Georgian Bay, which began operation November 30, 1858. He also had the longest career on the island, providing almost thirty-two years of service. His service was top-notch. The meticulous care he took in the upkeep and management of the lighthouse set a precedent for his successors.

Over 124 years, twelve men were responsible for keeping the light and protecting ships from the treacherous Mary Ward Shoals and Lockerbie Rock. A collection of their reminiscences, written by Marion Sandell in her book, *Keepers of the Light,* paints a vivid portrait of a lightkeeper's solitary life on the island. Often the lightkeepers' families would also live at Nottawasaga, in a residence just beside the lighthouse. While their parents kept busy with work, the children would find ingenious ways to pass the time. Thomas Foley's (keeper from 1924 to 1932) children made parachutes by tying rocks to the corners of their handkerchiefs then dropping them from the top of the lighthouse. They would sprint down the stairs, pick them up, race back up, and start all over again. No aerobic classes necessary here.

Usually there was an abundance of chores to keep idle hands busy - gathering water from the Bay, cutting the grass, chopping wood, or rowing for half a mile (.8 km) to get milk at a nearby farm. But there was also plenty of swimming, fishing, and snake-catching, not to mention the marshmallow roasts and card and board games at night. And everyone was taught how to run the light in case of emergency. The real reason they were on the island was never neglected.

When the light was automated in 1959, the Nottawasaga keepers no longer resided on the island, except for weekends or summer vacations. The island's underbrush quickly took over, and hundreds of birds - egrets, herons, cormorants, and gulls - started to make the island home. Over the past twenty years, a naturalist's

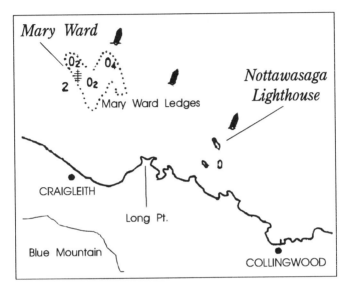

Refer to chart 2201

club and local supporters have been trying to convince Environment Canada and the Ministry of Transport to declare the island a migratory bird sanctuary. But according to Marion Sandell, they have been unsuccessful. As both an environmentally and historically important site, it is hoped that public awareness will soon make preservation and protection of Nottawasaga Island a reality.

The lighthouse stands alone on the northernmost point of the island, about three miles (4.8 km) northwest of Collingwood Harbour. The keeper's house, damaged by a 1959 fire and years of vandalism, was torn down in 1971. The island is owned and maintained by the

Canadian Coast Guard. Permission is needed to visit the site.

Meaford

You will pass the ports of Craigleith (see page 56), and Meaford standing at the mouth of Big Head River. The first log house, built by Peggy and David Miller in 1838, provided an important stopover for weary travelers. The site is now called Peggy's Landing. By 1840 their rest stop was joined by the obligatory watering hole - William Stephenson's tavern. Surrounding land was sold and the village began to emerge soon after. Like Collingwood, Meaford got its big break when the railway came to town. By 1865 the population had exploded to 1000. Meaford skipped the village stage, and became an official town in 1874. Its core consisted of eight hotels, two grist mills, two sawmills, two tanneries, two woolen mills, a foundry and a variety of shops. Meaford had its share of setbacks. A 1913 fire nearly decimated the entire town... or what was left of it, after the previous year's flood had swept away the power dam, flour mill, bridge, woollen Mill, tannery, and railway embankment.

Meaford Tank Range
Cape Rich Ghost Town

When entrepreneur Donald McLaren arrived in this area in 1852 to make his fortune, he had no way of knowing that the small "boom town" he was founding would continue that way. McLaren ran an early "gas station" on a wharf where he would supply steamers with hardwood fuel. Soon about 100 people were prospering in this village called St. Vincent. McLaren built a post office and general store that serviced the residents as well as the outlying fishing camps. As the hardwood supply dwindled, the town's focus shifted to the fishing industry and it soon became an active fishing base, producing over a thousand barrels of fish in one season, rivaling Collingwood. Like so many other towns on the Bay, however, it was only a matter of time before the fish stocks decreased. The town couldn't compete with other larger fishing centres that had rail access to the markets. People left and the town became quiet. Quiet until the Department of Defense bought the land — 10 miles (16km) across and five miles (8km) out from shore — for a firing range and used the old buildings of St. Vincent for tank target practice. It may be the only ghost town in Ontario to be blown up.

William Grenville Foley; Parachute game at the Nottawasaga Lighthouse.

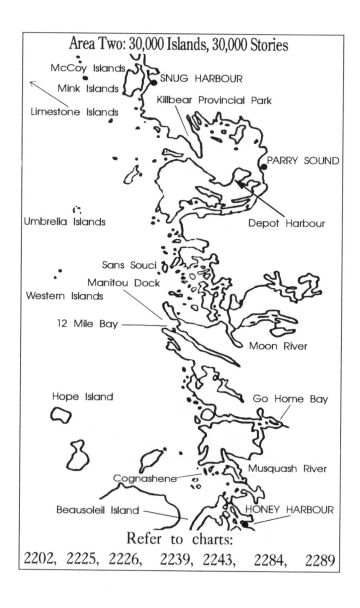

Area Two: 30,000 Islands, 30,000 Stories

McCoy Islands

SNUG HARBOUR

Mink Islands

Killbear Provincial Park

Limestone Islands

PARRY SOUND

Umbrella Islands

Depot Harbour

Sans Souci

Manitou Dock

Western Islands

12 Mile Bay

Moon River

Hope Island

Go Home Bay

Musquash River

Cognashene

Beausoleil Island

HONEY HARBOUR

Refer to charts:

2202, 2225, 2226, 2239, 2243, 2284, 2289

2

30,000 Islands, 30,000 Stories: The Eastern Shore

Like a flock of seagulls riding the prevailing wind, the stories and memories of the 30,000 Islands have a collective
spirit that soars. It floats over the rooftops of summer
homes in Honey Harbour and Cognashene, Sans Souci
and Parry Sound, and out over the craggy, windswept
islands, to the smooth pink granite of the Mink Islands. In
this area, serious ghost hunters will encounter the real
thing and find challenging mysteries to unravel. Here are
the stories of entrepreneurs boasting of their accomplish-
ments, fishermen spinning tales about "the big one", and
early cottagers laying down foundations and beginning
family legacies. Each voice that echoes through abandoned places and whispers in the crackling fire has a deep
connection to this great Bay.

For centuries, these broken shores, littered with

Parry Sound

shoals and islands, inhibited European exploration of Georgian Bay. Today, each resident works to conquer and memorize the hidden underwater dangers, and from this experience a deep appreciation and understanding of the Bay is born. Eras have come and gone, paddle wheelers and lavish summer resorts and hotels have long vanished, but the sense of community spirit engendered by shared experience has not wavered.

Many of these families have enjoyed Georgian Bay summers for over a century. The pull of the Bay must have been incredibly strong for the early pioneers. Roads were poor and in some areas non-existent. Travel by

horse-and-carriage was hardly a speedy mode of transportation. From Toronto to Georgian Bay could take up
to three days. Isolation and droves of mosquitoes and
blackflies must have further intimidated them. Yet, despite
the difficulties they came back year after year to drink in
the incredible beauty of these islands and to be rejuvinat-
ed.

Honey Harbour

North of Midland, Honey Harbour is one of the first cottage settlements on the Bay. Any old timer will describe
the anticipation that rose steadily on the slow train ride

Midland City and supplies en route

from the sweltering city and then the joy of feeling Georgian Bay's cool breezes on one's cheek. But to get from train to cottage required patience - and a ferry. A ferry that was passenger steamer, baggage transporter, post office as well as grocery delivery boy. Once en route her boilers fired at regular intervals and billows of black smoke trailed lazily behind. Some cottages in Honey Harbour date back to the turn of the century, and many of them had water access deep enough to allow direct dock delivery despite the *Midland City's* almost seven foot (2m) draft.

Cognashene

The history of Cognashene, a tightly-knit community with cottages dotting its islands, dates to the 1880s when the first residents staked their claims. Some were famous and some were not, but they all added colour. Each summer, the Cognashene locals mingled with the hundreds of tourists attracted to her summer resorts and beauty. One of the islands to most reflect the grandeur of this era was Minnicognashene Island.

Minnicognashene

It was a perfect summer day in 1955, except that a most difficult decision had to be made. All but three of the existing

Minnicog Hotel with its tower bedroom, 1920

original buildings on Minnicognashene had to be burned down for safety reasons. Nearby residents gathered on their islands while others drifted close to Minnicog in their boats. They had come to bid a final farewell. As intense flames exploded through tinder-dry walls, black smoke carried away the spirit of an entire era. In minutes the grand hotel, and its surrounding cottages, cabins, and annexes were gone. Years of Minnicog tradition vanished. One woman reminisced of coming to Minnicog on three separate occasions, each time enjoying the same Sunday brunch of roast beef au jus, pineapple sherbet, and assorted cakes - not a spectacular memory, really, until you realize that the visits spanned a full thirty years.

Circling around the island, we tried to imagine the resort in the 1920's, when it accommodated as many as 250 guests. In the twilight we could almost see two horses and a cart bringing the late arrivals' baggage up from the dock. Dinner had long been served and the kitchen staff was giving the scraps to the pigs. The sun cropped by the horizon, stretched its fiery fingers to feather the tips of the waves. A few guests lingered to enjoy the sunset but some, anticipating the dance, had retired to change into their evening wear. Three boys in suit jackets and ties paddled along the shore listening to the band rehearse. Others relaxed on the verandah sipping Tom Collins' as they watched the last couples finishing their match on the wooden plank tennis court. The bowling green was still being used by the family staying out on the far tent plat-form. The sun was now only a sliver, and it was time to lower the flag. Another day had come to an end on Minnicognashene.

Life on the island continued in this grand style for many years, until more and more vacationers bought their own land and built their own cottages. Sue Russell writes about the hotel's decline, in an article, "A History of Minnicognashene", in the 1979 *Cognashene Cottager*. In 1937, the hotel was still open but not economically viable. The depression had its effect, and many regular guests could no longer afford to come. Many others "vigorously upheld" their vacation tradition, even when they could not pay their bills. In 1938 it was bought for $11,000 by a group of islanders and long-time guests for use as a private club. It thrived until 1941, when many of the male mem-bers went off to war. Herbert C. Jarvis, who held the mort-

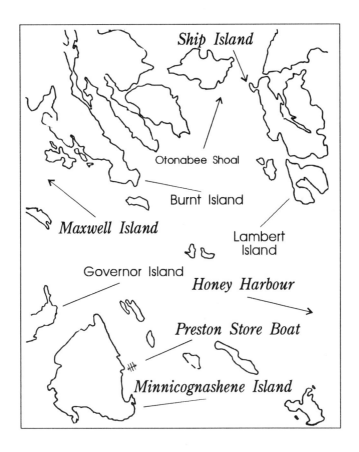

Refer to charts   2202, 2239

gage, paid the owners one dollar for the island then resold it for one dollar to the Navy League, who used it as a summer training camp for Sea Cadets. They too found it a financial burden, and the camp closed after eight years. While it lay vacant, a caretaker made a tidy profit selling off the hand-carved oak furniture and the dining room dishes. In 1955, a battered Minnicog was bought by Robert Jarvis, who reluctantly decided it must be razed.

The Preston's Store Boat Wreck

If the cottagers missed getting their grocery order delivered onto the *Midland City* steamer, the *Preston's Store* Boat was every mother's second chance for food. Cottagers and hotels in Cognashene enjoyed this delivery service for years - until August 1934, when the twenty-eight ton gasoline launch caught fire. A small ribbed section of her hull remained on the shore of Minnicognashene Island's east side for years and marked the spot where the main body of the wreck lay in about ten feet (3m) of water. *NOTE: If you are diving or snorkeling on the wreck do so from a boat as Minnicognashene Island is privately owned.*

Lambert Island
Orville Wright

During the 1920s and 30s, a most distinguished American, Orville Wright, resided on Lambert Island. Along with his brother, Wilbur, Orville was the first to invent and take flight in a powered aeroplane. Orville was known as a gentle, soft-spoken man who dressed up in a suit with a starched Arrow collar and bow tie even on the hottest of days. His sailing prowess was legendary. While trying to master his new dingy, he was watched by locals as a strong breeze caught his sail. Out of control, and unsure of what to do, he let the boat ram up onto the beach so hard that it became tangled in the deep underbrush. With slightly tousled hair, Mr. Wright stepped out of the boat and addressed the gaping crowd with his usual calm dignity, "Now you can see why I was made an honorary member of the Minnicog Yacht Club."

One mystery about Orville Wright stands out - his relationship with his sister Katherine. They were deeply committed to one another and believed they should sacrifice everything towards the invention of their aeroplane, the Kitty Hawk. Katherine contributed her earnings and vowed, as did Orville, not to marry until the Kitty Hawk was a success. Years later, after the brothers achieved fame for their pioneering flights, Katherine announced to Orville that she was to be married. He never forgave her, and she never returned to Georgian Bay.

Musquash River

Most of the names, stories and legends in this area hark back to the great lumbering days. Ship Island was so named to remind sailors traveling from the mill towns down to Penetanguishene to favour its shores in order to avoid deadly contact with Otonabee Shoal.

The colourful legend of lumberman Sandy Gray captures the true spirit of the Musquash River area (locally referred to as the Muskoka River.) Located at the river's mouth was the early mill town of Muskoka Mills (1867-1895), home to the Muskoka Milling and Lumber Company (1875-1895), and many less-than-refined loggers. Their boss, the leader of the Musquash gang, was Sandy Gray. One Sunday, a log jam on the river was slowing production. With an unyielding determination, Gray broke the Sabbath and said "Boys, we'll break the jam or breakfast in hell." Gray, unknown to himself, was a prophet. He managed to free the jam but the logs broke so quickly they carried him over a waterfall to his death. The Falls bear his name to this day.

Muskoka Mills

Muskoka Mills was a company village that existed from 1867 to 1895. During its boom period there were five mills (bought in 1875 by the Muskoka Milling and Lumber Company) and about twenty houses, a schoolhouse with a church room on top, and a guest house called the "Rossin House." Twenty to thirty foot (6 to 9m) docks stretched along the shoreline. The main docks, to which eleven tugs, and numerous scows and barges could be tied, extended approximately 800 yards (720 m) into the Bay.

Records show that the mill was charged in 1884 for unsound environmental practices. The ravages of the mill can still be found in the aptly named Sawdust Bay. When we pressed our paddles into the shallows, we were astounded at the depth of the sawdust that still chokes the

Muskoka Mills

water. The mills' refuse poured furiously into the water through water-powered troughs. Besides sawdust, the lake bottom is still littered with boards and cribs. As if this evidence of pollution were not enough, there is the story of a bizarre fire that began in some buildings, appeared to be out and then reignited several times years later. There was so much refuse and sawdust that the fire was able to smolder underground undetected. Many felt this proved that Sandy Gray was still breakfasting in hell. *NOTE: When heading up the Musquash River it is best to travel in a small outboard, or paddle in a canoe, as the river depth varies and it is full of lumber and other concealed navigational hazards. Be sure to stay in the middle of the river.*

The Wales Wreck

This wreck is easy to find and quite visible from the surface. The site is ideal for snorkeling and the morning light offers a good view of her large hull resting in 10 to 20 feet (3m to 6m) of water.

The *Wales*, a 238-ton-tug built in 1864 in Brockville, Ontario, was owned by the Chaffy Brothers Company and later sold to Louis Hotchkiss, reportedly an owner of one of the five largest lumber operations in North America. Hotchkiss in turn sold the sturdy tug to Hughson & Company, where she served the Muskoka Mills from 1881 until 1895. When her twenty-one years began to show, she was deemed unseaworthy and was abandoned on the east side of Longuissa Point in Longuissa Bay.

The Chippewa Wreck

Another workhorse of the Muskoka Mills was launched in 1874, as the 132-ton *Chippewa*. She spent three decades in the company's service commuting mostly to Sarnia and by 1905, she was worn out. Like the *Wales*, she was sunk the following year in the Musquash River less than a mile (1.3 km) upstream from the southern end of Longuissa Point. She is located off the west bank of the river, just past two rocks near the river widening (see map.) Her hull is still intact, lying in three to ten feet (0.9m to 3 m) of water. *NOTE: Strong river currents, heavy boating traffic, and poor visibility can be hazardous.*

The Ontario Wreck

This wooden barge spent many years in the timber trade like its sisters the *Wales* and the *Chippewa*, and was abandoned in the river due to old age. The *Ontario* lies about three-quarters of a mile (1.2km) upstream from the *Chippewa* close to the river bank, just below the second set of rapids. The wreck is in a sheltered spot but care

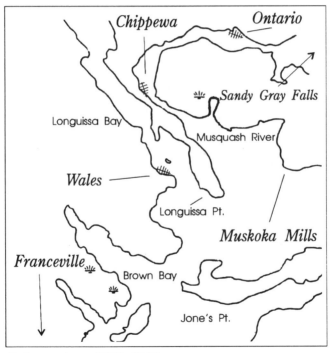

Refer to charts 2202, 2239

Franceville : Some say it was the success of the Rossin Guest House at Muskoka Mills that inspired Williams France's family to build the first of their several hotels near "Freddie Channel" in 1895. They created a local landmark called Franceville, where they served up meals, friendship, and sound advice.

should be taken when passing the first set of rapids — keep to starboard. The wreck is easily visible from the surface. Snorkeling is all that is necessary to enjoy this relaxing site which stands in 10 to 20 feet (3m to 6m) of water.

Maxwell Island/Whalen Island

Grandma Whalen of Penetanguishene was desperate to seek relief from the severe hay fever and chronic asthma which troubled her in town. She asked permission of the Muskoka Mills Lumbering Company to stay with her invalid son on what was then called Maxwell Island, where the company operated a wharf on the northeastern shore. The owners saw no reason to refuse. After all, what could a little old woman do? From the beginning it was apparent that Grandma might have been little but was not weak spirited. To ensure that snakes would not "partake in her convalescence" she calmly sprinkled salt around her tent.

Over time, thanks to the fresh air and her newly-

Whalen Island Summer House

Grandma Whalen

acquired strength, Grandma turned her talents to property development. First the little tent was transformed into a small cottage. In 1902, the cottage burned. But for Grandma, this was not devastation, this was a sign - time to expand! She picked a more picturesque location and built a larger summer house. By now the word was out about the healing properties of the Bay. Asthma sufferers began pilgrimages to Maxwell Island. By 1912, Cognashene was flourishing and passenger boats began regular routes past the island. Grandma sniffed opportunity and built an addition plus an annex to the house - and so began the famous Whalen Island Summer House for tourists. Wealthy and distinguished guests arrived followed by pigs, cows and chickens, and a store, and a post office. Sadly, the big house was destroyed by fire in 1942, but Grandma's descendants still enjoy the island and still laugh about her indomitable spirit.

Go Home Bay

One local explained that the name Go Home Bay came from the natives. When they traded inland by canoe, they passed through Go Home Bay before traversing the open water to return home.

Before the advent of refrigeration, summer residents of Go Home Bay used sawdust from the Muskoka Mills to ensure that the ice in their icehouses remained cool and dry during the hot months. There were only a few motor boats in the area and owners could be identified by the distinctive sounds of their one-or-two-cylinder engines knocking along. These engines were temperamental and more than one old-timer tells of being stranded overnight on a rock compliments of a broken motor. Unreliability, however, was not confined to small boats. One salty old captain of the *City of Toronto*, who had never gained a love for Go Home Bay's rocky channel, was rather irritated to learn that he was making this tricky trip to deliver only two items: a young man and a dinghy. Not known for his subtlety, the captain slowed the steamer, set the displeased boy and dinghy afloat and told him to find his own way home. One wonders if he even bothered to glance back as he chugged off on his route. (For more on this old steamer see p. 5.)

One of the finest legacies to come out of Cognashene

and Go Home Bay was the distinct artistic vision of A.Y. Jackson, one of Canada's Group of Seven painters. Jackson spent much of his later years capturing on canvas images of Go Home Bay. He wrote of being amazed at how he could return year after year and always find new subjects to paint. Even locations that did not initially interest him could suddenly be transformed under a new play of Georgian Bay light.

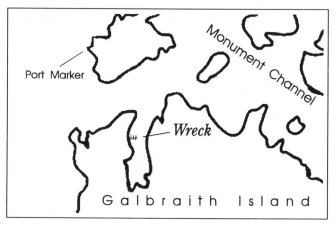

Refer to chart 2202, sheet 2

Galbraith Island Tug Wreck

Little is known about this wreck except that it is a good site for snorkeling. The unidentified tug lies off the northeast corner of Galbraith Island in ten feet (3m) of water. The site is in a calm cove close to the small boat channel and includes her broken keel, about 55 feet (16.5m) long, and surrounding pieces of frame and other timber. *NOTE: Please swim out to the wreck from your boat, as the island is privately owned.*

W.J. Martin Wreck

The *Martin* spent only two months on the Bay before she burned at Long Bay in November 1905, making her the vessel with the shortest life in Georgian Bay navigational history. The 75-foot (22.5m) hull of this wooden steamer lies in about 5 to 25 feet (1.5 to 7.5m) of water at Middle Rock, between Ward and Fairlie Islands, adjacent to the small boat channel. There is a marker next to the wreck. The highlight of the Martin dive is her creepy, dark boiler. The site is good for both diving and snorkeling.

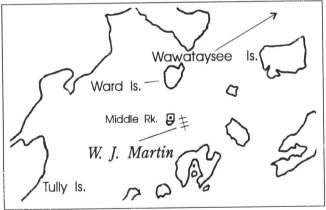

Refer to chart 2202, sheet 2

Manitou Dock

The Manitou Dock, like dozens of other public docks up and down the islands, served as a "town square" where supplies and mail were delivered, and the latest gossip was exchanged. When peering through the pristine water, watching bass dart through vestiges of cribs and old spikes, it is hard to imagine the giant steamers, the life blood of the communities, landing at docks such as this all over the Bay: the *Waubuno* (see story); the *Manitoulin*, later the *Atlantic* (see   story); the *Chicoutimi*; the

Go Home Bay steamer dock. "Town Square"

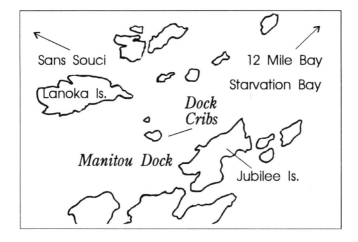

Refer to chart 2202, sheet 3

Maxwell; *SS Brittanic*; *SS Waubic*; *Midland City* (see p5); the *City of Dover*; and many others. But there were times they failed to land. For steamboat racing had spread from the Mississippi River to the Great Lakes, and now, when rival steamers had the same route, a race most surely ensued. Such was the case when the *Pacific* was lagging behind the *Cambria*. The *Pacific* skipped her stops at Kagawong and Serpent River and only tucked in at Richard's Landing long enough for two agitated business-men to leap to the dock.

The Waubuno Mystery

The *Waubuno*, a 120-foot (36 m) side-wheeler, blazed her route from Collingwood to Parry Sound. On November 21, 1879, she was moored due to a storm. Passengers became increasingly anxious with each wave that slapped against the windows. Their unease was heightened by a foreboding rumour. It seems that a young bride, the wife of Dr. Doupe, had recounted a dream in which she saw the *Waubuno* ripped apart in a horrific storm, and her passengers tossed into the deep. As Mrs. Doupe struggled to keep her head above water, she witnessed the terrified expressions of the others as they were swallowed by the cold, black water. She begged to leave the ship. Her husband tried to calm her, reasoning that all their furniture and belongings for their new home and his new practice at McKellar Village were already loaded on board. She unwillingly agreed and returned to her berth.

The story was upsetting a lot of people. Those less-superstitious reminded the others that Captain Burkett was an experienced seaman who could "smell a rock a mile away," and that he was "presently playing it safe" as the *Waubuno* and the *Magnetawan* sat out the fierce northwest gale in Collingwood Harbour. The *Waubuno* had an "excellent track record, not a serious problem in fourteen years of service." "She was getting old," countered another passenger, and was now under great pressure to compete with the sleek and speedy new *Magnetawan*. "And you know," offered another passenger with a twinkle in his eye, "in the Algonkin language, "Waubuno" means black art or black magic." Some people

The Waubuno. A passenger had a premonition of the steamers's demise.

chuckled - most were silent.

By late evening, it was apparent the storm would continue throughout the night. Many passengers took rooms at the Globe Hotel close to the docks. About 4 a.m., the storm subsided and the eager captain told his crew to prepare for an early morning departure. Some say he blew the steamer's whistle to signal to the passengers in the hotel; some say he sent a purser, but no one was willing to leave their warm bed; others say he deliberately left without them, as in, "you leave my boat, you don't deserve to come back on." Whatever one believes, the fact is the passengers at the Globe were thankful they didn't make it onto the *Waubuno* that cold wintry morning. Captain Burkett pulled out of Collingwood with twenty-four people on board. The *Magnatewan* delayed her departure.

Shortly, the winds rose and it began to snow heavily. The Christian Island lightkeeper noted in his log "stiff wind from the nor'west but ship seemed to be riding well with full cargo." A second vessel taking shelter from the storm around Hope Island reported seeing the *Waubuno* rolling in the heavy seas with no signs of stopping. Around noon, two loggers on the Moon River thought they heard a steamer's faint distress signal. The *Magnetewan* arrived in Parry Sound two days later. She had not seen the *Waubuno* during her journey. The Parry Sound Lumber Company's *Mittie Grew* was sent out to look for her.

At first, all the *Mittie Grew* found was a crushed lifeboat close to Copperhead Island, a paddlebox, freight, and shattered pieces of the Doupe's furniture and other debris scattered along the islands off the South Channel. Later they spotted life preservers, all of them accounted for. It appeared that no one had even had a chance to put one on.

The next spring, the *Waubuno*'s upturned hull was discovered in a little bay near Wreck Island, about seven miles (11.2 km) off the steamer's course. But still no bodies were found. A few years later fishermen started bringing pieces of the wreckage up in their nets: a passenger trunk, chains, and bits of freight. In the 1950s and 1960s, divers started to comb the area. They brought up her big anchor (now in Waubuno Park in Parry Sound,) a captain's pistol and rolls of Waubuno Notes, "money" the Beatty family periodically used at their company stores. In the 1960s, John Morris may have discovered a part of the superstructure poking up from the silt. It was eight to ten feet (2.34 to 3m) long with two-inch (5cm) oak decking on three-by-six inch (7.5x15cm) beams. Unfortunately, when Morris surfaced, his boat had vanished and he drifted aimlessly for hours until he was finally picked up by a passerby. Every attempt to later relocate the spot was unsuccessful. Morris felt that a strong undertow must have shifted the silt to reveal the Waubuno then moved it back to again hide the ship.

Theories abound about how the *Waubuno* foundered. Some say the ship sank near Sandy Island; some believe the hull in Wreck Island Cove is not the *Waubuno*'s as it is the wrong size, and that the wreck is intact near Lone Rock, sitting upright on the bottom. The most probable explanation is that Captain Burkett was seeking shelter. Miscalculating, he hit a shoal just southwest of the Haystack Rocks and dropped anchor. The wind, snow and waves capsized the vessel, trapping all the passengers and crew. The hull ripped away from the passenger deck and floated to Wreck Island where it was discovered by a man named Pedonquot in March 1880. The passenger deck, with its precious human cargo disappeared into the depths.

Just north of Wreck Island in a calm inlet on the southern tip of Bradden Island lies the *Waubuno* hull in less than 14 feet (4.5m) of water. Her intact keel is home to pike, bass, and perch, and the site is good for both snorkeler and diver. The more adventurous can try combing the open water southwest of the Haystack Rocks in an attempt to solve one of the Bay's most guarded secrets.

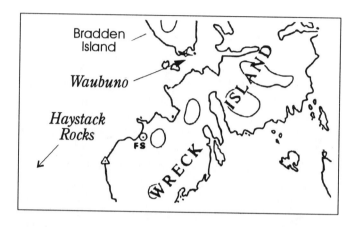

Refer to chart 2202, sheet 3

Western Islands

About fifteen miles (24km) across open water from the site of the *Waubuno*'s hull are the Western Islands: a remote sanctuary for seagulls who soar and shriek overhead. Their unique folded rock formations are carpeted in yellow lichen - the north group of islands are especially beautiful. Today the Westerns can make you feel you're visiting the ends of the earth, but they were not always this desolate. Fishermen used to frequent the area and a lighthouse keeper maintained a lonely vigil. *Island Odyssey*, published by the Sans Souci and Copperhead Association

The Western Islands Lighthouse

tells about one fisherman, Teddy Norris, a local scallywag who discovered a spot off the Westerns he called the "Musk Hole" where trout were huge and plentiful. Teddy and his workmate Archie Cunningham had a routine: out to "the big hole," drop the nets, return to the abandoned fishing shanties for an overnight stay (made more pleasant by a visit with the lighthouse keeper and a bottle of whisky.) In the morning, the catch was lifted, and the fish were cleaned and the nets mended on the way back to Midland. Later, the two would divide the cash - some towards necessities, and the rest towards replenishing the whisky stocks.

The lighthouse and it's keeper made the Westerns a favorite spot for local cottagers, who often brought food in exchange for his yarns about the Bay. For a good loaf of bread you might hear his favourite: the story of the burly Captain Henman who bragged about surviving four decades on the Bay and four shipwrecks. After visiting the keeper on the Westerns he continued on his journey only to be caught in a fierce gale. Henman's lifeboat was found bobbing near the shore of Christian Island but neither his body, nor the $1,500 in cash the Western's keeper had seen him carrying was ever found. Now all that remain on the Westerns are the main light, walkways, and the coal pit which was probably in the basement of the former light-keeper's house. Pick a "good-weather" day on which to visit the Westerns, as being caught in a storm out here would not be a pleasant experience(see Atlantic story).

Copperhead Island

The tinkling of a piano could often be heard, especially if it was a lazy summer evening and the wind was warm and the moon was bright and people felt like dancing. On such nights people from miles around would come to the Copperhead Hotel for an evening of entertainment.

This fashionable hotel began as a fishing camp in the early 1880s, run by the brothers Archie and Johnny Campbell. As more upscale tourists were attracted to the area, the fishing camp developed into a resort, the Campbell House. Rates for the 55 guests were $1.50 to $2.00 a day or $10 to $12 a week. Most summers the resort was full.

Copperhead Island, Georgian Bay, Canada.

Copperhead Hotel

But tragedy struck Copperhead Island in 1912, when Archie Campbell died suddenly at the helm of his boat. His brother tried but failed to run Campbell House and in 1915 was forced to sell. The new owners renamed her the Copperhead Hotel. A year later it was sold again and renamed The Light House. Guests fished, sailed, and swam. They eagerly awaited the arrival of the *Midland City* every evening at 6:30, bringing more guests and mail. The weekly visit from the *City of Dover*, dropped off fresh meat and vegetables, dried goods and better, tobacco and candy. At night they would play cards, dance, sing, or take moonlit walks along the shore.

Cottages sprang up on the islands around

Copperhead. Since there were no phones, electricity or cruisers, many of the cottages were built facing the hotel. If there was trouble, they could signal the hotel with a lantern or cowbell. Cottagers relied on The Light House for more than just security: they would scoot over in their row boats whenever they needed ice or ran out of milk, thus qualifying her as probably the first cornerstore in the community.

Tragedy struck the resort in 1937, when owner Elijah Light drowned in a boating accident. The family stayed on for another decade but eventually sold the hotel in 1950 to Howard Vaughan who renamed her the Copperhead Hotel. The Copperhead's streak of bad luck was not yet over. A violent storm destroyed the docks and boathouse. Vaughan didn't have the money for the repairs, and the Copperhead became run down. In 1954, Vaughan employed the Pinkneys to manage the hotel - they spruced her up and kept her going until 1962 when it was time to face the truth. No amount of paint and new nails could hide the fact that the Copperhead was too old and too costly to be maintained. Her time had come.

For years she defied the Bay's winds and storms but it was the hands of vandals that finally wore her down. She was a lonely, eerie sight for the twenty-odd years that she stood empty, the wind blowing bedroom doors open and closed, mice nesting in the beds and occasionally banging out an off-key note or two as they scampered across the yellowing piano keys. A cottager eventually rescued the piano and others converted parts of the verandah into bed frames and other useful items. The Copperhead was demolished in 1988, one year shy of her 100th birthday.

All that is left are some rotting dock cribs, a crumbling incinerator, and two smaller buildings: the store/post office and a guest house (now used as a summer cottage.) The island is privately owned but from the water you can visualize where the hotel stood. Below the surface you may find mementos from the Copperhead's past scattered along the cribbing. It is pleasant to snorkel and dive among the piles of debris from yesteryear: motors, pots, and coal from the *Midland City*. Divers beware, however, not everything you find may be authentic. The Vaughan's grandchildren once shared a good laugh at the expense of a naive diver. They watched as he stole away from his companions to open a strange, tightly wrapped box he had retrieved from the water. One can imagine his expression when he found only an old doll inside. Months before, the children had performed a funeral and tossed the doll and her coffin into the Bay.

Jumbo Island

Across the Bay from Copperhead is Jumbo Island, ironically named after a sickly young man who lived here with his family in the 1880s. It was hoped that clean air and pure water would strengthen his lungs. It seemed to do the trick as he grew to be a strapping young man of six-foot, six inches, nicknamed, of course, Jumbo. Years later, a white elephant was painted on the northeast side of the island to commemorate the story. On a more practical note, area residents also use it to measure the water level of the Bay each year.

Refer to chart 2202, sheet 3

Sans Souci Hotel and Area

Four gentlemen in pinstriped cotton suits stroll down the pier to share a cigar and await the approaching *City of Toronto*. On the verandah the women, in their long dresses and wide brimmed hats, await the return of their husbands from fishing. Their laughter mixes with the sound of the squawking gulls following behind the advancing steamer. A scene from The Great Gatsby? No, just another lovely day at the Sans Souci Hotel.

The Sans Souci area has always been somewhat of a meeting place, as many early fishing clubs grew up on her shores. But it was not until 1894 when entrepreneur John

The Sans Souci Hotel

Pearce built the first hotel on the island that it was established as the area's social centre. He named the hotel after Champlain's apt description of this region, *"sans souci,"* without care.

An article in the 1973 annual cottage report by the late E.I. Phillips recalls Sans Souci as a substantial operation consisting of two separate structures, a hotel and a dining hall. In addition there was also a store, post office, large boathouse, laundry facility, pump house, and ice house. Inside the hotel there were bedrooms with a common bathroom at the end of the hall. A fireplace at the bottom of the stairs provided warmth on cold days.

The Hotel had its share of tall tales. When the infa-

Teddy Norris

mous Teddy Norris (see Western Islands story) was caretaker, a serious fire started in the dining hall. Teddy's
deadpan explanation was "spontaneous combustion." But
Teddy had a good heart. Wanting to put a scorched shoe
that was salvaged from the rubble to good use, he sent it
off to a man on Moose Deer Point who had only one leg.
Teddy was pleased to learn it was a perfect fit.

In the 1930s, hotel businesses suffered. Sans Souci
proved no exception. With the untimely death of owner
William McArthur, rumoured to have accidentally killed
himself while cleaning a gun, the hotel was shut down and
abandoned. Once the centre of the area's activity, the Sans
Souci was now a deserted monument to a vibrant past. In

1946, the Sans Souci Hotel was torn down, leaving only a few hooks in the rock and some cribbing off the island's shores.

Despite the loss of the hotel, the Sans Souci community united and the centre merely shifted across the channel to Frying Pan Island. In 1927, the Sans Souci cottagers merged with the Copperhead cottagers to form the Sans Souci-Copperhead Association, which now operates out of an old schoolhouse. Together with a dozen other associations, it is officially recognized as part of the Township of Archipelago, giving the cottagers and residents a voice in the development and future of the area. On Frying Pan Island the Township of San Souci is also still very much the centre of activity in this part of the Bay, offering boating services at the government dock and nearby marina. Here also stand monuments dedicated to the seventeenth-century explorers Samuel de Champlain and René-Robert Cavelier de La Salle who passed through the area.

Massasauga Provincial Park

Sans Souci has as much to attract visitors as it did in 1894. It is a boater's paradise, a labyrinth of beautiful islands and inviting coves. Part of Sans Souci overlaps the adjacent 29,000 acre (11,000 ha) Massasauga Provincial Park which offers an astounding variety of earth and life science features including old logging and fishing camps and mines. According to the Park's management plan, its goal is to "protect the unique natural landscapes and heritage resources of the Park, while providing complementary educational and water-based recreation opportunities for present and future generations." Camping, boating, hiking, fishing, canoeing, and cross-country skiing are available. Also in the area are the thirty foot (9m) Moon River Falls.

Umbrella Islands

Navigating the Umbrellas is quite tricky, as high waves pound in from the open Bay, and treacherous channels hide nasty rocks. Inconsistent water levels add to the challenge. The reward is breathtaking scenery and dramatic atmosphere. These low smooth rocks offer a great hideaway. Only the remains of a few fishing shanties and dock cribs, and a handful of seagulls kept us company as we settled back to watch the vibrant sunset.

Emma Wreck

We were permitted by the ever gracious historian Dave Thomas to see a turn-of-the-century treasure from his archive. The yellowed pages of little Vera Hays' diary gave us a child's vision of the steamer *Emma*. "*Emma* was a little trim craft that made at least two trips a day from Parry Sound and stopping at Rose Point and Parry Harbour. We'd edge past the opening where we could see a little man dancing on the throbbing engine, go through the cabin with its red velvet upholstered seats and if it was a fine day we would go up on deck. There was a music box

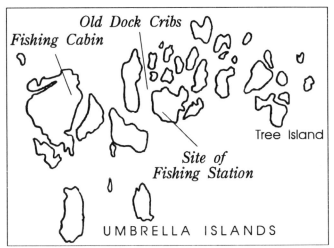

Old Dock Cribs
Fishing Cabin
Tree Island
Site of
Fishing Station
UMBRELLA ISLANDS

Refer to chart 2224

in the cabin and Captain Pratt ran her."

The 89-foot (26.7-m) steam yacht was built in Collingwood by Robert J. Morrill in 1894, then enlarged in 1901 in Parry Sound for the passenger trade. She served both locals and tourists for eleven years until July 4, 1912, when she was sent across the Bay to help out with tourist traffic at the King's Royal Hotel in Owen Sound. The *Emma* caught fire just off the outer channels of Parry Sound and burned to the waterline; there was no loss of life.

Only the hull of the *Emma* can be found at this site, as her boiler and engine were salvaged after World War I. She can be found in 4 to 20 feet (1.2m to 6m) of water in a sheltered cove about a half a mile from Sister Rock Beacon off the Boyd Group of Islands.

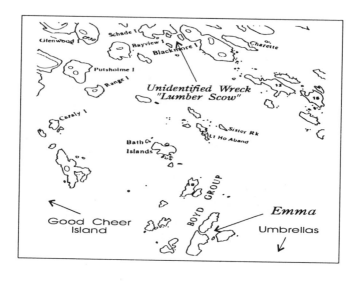

Refer to chart 2205, sheet 3

Unnamed Schooner

One of the most peaceful experiences on Georgian Bay is
a morning swim, which can be made even more interesting by snorkeling on this unnamed wreck. This small scow
(probably another abandoned workhorse for the lumber
trade) lies in 10 to 15 feet (3 to 4.5m) of water just east of
Blackmore Island and just west of a smallcraft channel. It
is a good site for the first-time snorkeler and can be
viewed from above by those who don't relish the early
morning dip.

Emma, with her velvet seats and music box

Good Cheer Island

The islands surrounding Good Cheer belong to the Boyds, one of the first cottaging families in the area. As early as 1881, John Alexander Boyd took his five eldest sons from Toronto to Georgian Bay. One day while paddling around in a rented rowboat, they were surprised by a freak storm and took shelter. Mr. Boyd cracked open a bottle of whiskey, and as they all shared a swig, he grinned "Well boys, this is a little bit of Good Cheer," thus christening the island for generations to come.

Back then it was no weekend jaunt to the Bay. The Boyds stayed from June until Thanksgiving, and the large family was tended by quite an entourage: a cook, handyman, engineer, maid, laundress, and nursemaid. During the 1800s, Good Cheer Island was home to a rather rowdy fishing camp. On Saturday nights when the nets were drying, the men imbibed a bit of their own "good cheer." More than once a drunken temper broke into a brawl, and fists turned to knives. The Boyd family would be sick with worry when Mr. Boyd rowed over to arbitrate a little peace back into the Georgian Bay summer night.

Parry Sound

If someone had told William Beatty Jr., MA and LLB that he would abandon his potentially great career in law and politics to found a hole-in-the-rock town on the northeastern shores of Georgian Bay, he would have laughed. He was only going out for the afternoon with his brother and brother-in-law to help his father look for timber rights in this newly prosperous area.

They set out one morning in 1863 only to have their prospecting trip cut short by a small storm that drove them to seek shelter in Parry Sound. As fate would have it, surveyor William Gibson had just put his mill, located on the Seguin River, a few cabins, and his surrounding timber rights up for sale. The Beattys who had liked what they saw in Parry Sound quickly bought the package. Beatty Jr. was so enamoured with the area and its potential that he stayed on, becoming the resident manager for the family and the driving force behind the new town.

Beatty Jr. made a success of the mill and bought up the surrounding lands. He also dabbled in the shipping industry, helping the family's Northwest Navigational Company of Sarnia, a.k.a. the Beatty Line, by building their first steamer, the *Waubuno*, in 1865 for freight and passenger service out of Parry Sound. In 1867, he bought the Parry Sound town site and began to lay out plans for housing his workers and buildings for necessary support services. Beatty was a staunch Wesleyan Methodist and a member of the Reform Party, who thought he could set the moral code for his own town. Using his skills as a lawyer and politician he introduced the "Beatty covenant," which prohibited the sale or trade of liquor on any of his properties, thus ensuring everyone in church on Sunday would be of sober mind and body. The church had also been built by Beatty, who sometimes conducted his own services. The covenant only seemed to upset a few of the residents, who moved elsewhere. It was enforced until 1950 when the Provincial Legislature withdrew the restriction.

With the town and his business under control, Beatty took time to dabble in one of his first loves, politics. In 1867, he ran as a member of Parliament for the Algoma District against a M.W. Simpson from Owen Sound. Both men and their numerous supporters traveled by separate steamers up to the polls at Sault Ste. Marie; Beatty on the *Waubuno*, Simpson on the *Algoma*. Unfortunately the *Waubuno* experienced engine trouble and by the time they arrived, the polling station was closed. Simpson had won by a handful of votes. Despite the defeat the townspeople of Parry Sound fondly referred to Beatty as the

William Beatty Jr.

"Governor" for years.

Throughout the 1860s, Beatty continued to build up his mills, keeping his lumberjacks busy. But all that work was making them thirsty and living under the heat of the Beatty covenant did nothing to quench their thirst. In 1873, the Guelph Lumber Company built a large mill on the eastern bank of the Seguin River just out of reach of the covenant. A new village, complete with hotel and tavern, sprang up. Officially, it was called Parry Harbour then Codrington, but it quickly earned the nickname, "Parry Hoot" due to the excessive hootin' and hollarin' heard for miles around. Liquor poured freely into the mouths of the loggers and the hell-raising tom-foolery spilled out, earning Parry Hoot the reputation as one of the rowdiest towns on the Bay, even more so than Corkscrew City (see Owen Sound.)

Beatty turned a deaf ear to the Hoot and continued to turn a tidy profit on all his investments. In 1872, he had bought out both his brother and father and was now sole proprietor of the Beatty interests in Parry Sound. He married and settled into a comfortable life in the town that he built.

Today Parry Sound is one of five cities on Georgian Bay and the only city on the northeastern shore. During the summer it boasts a wide range of tourist attractions: For three weeks in the summer the Festival of Sound brings music to the city. The new West Parry Sound District Museum, adjacent to the gardens and historic lookout tower overlooking Parry Sound and its waterways, tells the stories of the people who have influenced the area. Natives, explorers, trappers, lumberjacks, steamboat crews, settlers, entrepreneurs, and long-time cottagers are all represented. Boat tours and hiking tours are also available.

Unnamed Wreck and the Ella Ross

While in the Parry Sound area there are a number of dive sites to see. An unidentified 138-foot (41.4m) sailing ship lies in less than 10 feet (3m) of water in the shallows northwest of Oak Island. It's a nice shallow, sheltered dive that both snorkelers and divers will enjoy. For sailboat aficionados, note the wreck's offset centreboard and her

Steamer South America at Parry Sound

maststeps built around and over the keel rather than into it. Her rudder is visible near the stern.

For information in locating the wrecks of the *George H. Jones*, which caught fire and sank near Parry Sound October 4, 1917; the *Northwind*, a steamer that sank at the entrance of Parry Sound Harbour July 1, 1926; the *Ophir*, which burned in Parry Sound Harbour May 27, 1919; and the 99-foot (29.7m) paddlewheeler passenger vessel, the *Ella Ross*, which burned to the waterline at the wharf on June 9, 1912 and stands in twenty feet (6m) of water, enquire at the Parry Sound dive shop.

Parry Sound Harbour

Depot Harbour

The bartender smiled to himself as he polished the last of the shotglasses and laid them on a shelf above the bar. The hotel owner whistled cheerfully as he rolled a large barrel of whisky from the stockroom. Their eyes met knowingly. Things were going to get even better in Parry Hoot. You see, a new town was being built just four miles (7 km) south of Parry Sound, and rumour had it that its proprietor, some lumber gent from Ottawa name of Booth, was just as uptight as that Beatty fella' in Parry Sound. Like Beatty, he didn't want any booze on the town premises.

The bartender made a mental note to order more whisky.

In Ottawa, J.R. Booth owned lumber mills and had interests in the railway, strategically piecing together rail access to the ice-free Atlantic ports for his mills. By 1883, Booth began to expand into the grain trade. All he needed was a port and the men to run it. In 1891, Booth bought into the troubled Parry Sound Colonization Railway intending to connect it to his already thriving rail network. This would mean that all the cargo shipped into Parry Sound Harbour could be directly delivered to the Atlantic by rail. The benefits to Parry Sound would be immeasurable. Booth put out the word that he was looking to buy land for this railway, but the responses received enraged him. The Parry Sound landowners had asked top dollar for their land. Booth dissolved relations and left Parry Sound in a huff. He would show them how business was done.

It didn't take him long to find a superior port to Parry Sound. About four miles (7km) south, on Parry Island, was Canada's largest freshwater harbour with a flat back shore, just waiting for Booth to discover - or had he discovered it already? Historians have strong evidence Booth never intended to do business in Parry Sound, he just used the early partnership to gain government subsidies. Booth announced brazenly in the local paper that he would be building his rail terminus on Parry Island. This was news to the Ojibwa who lived there and owned the land. But Booth knew something the Ojibwa didn't - the law. He found a nasty piece of legislation that allowed for the appropriation of native land for rail purposes. In 1895, the Ojibwa of Parry Island were forced to sell their 314.5

J. R. Booth

acres (125.8 ha) for $9 an acre. Booth was in business and Parry Sound was not.

In 1896-97, Booth amalgamated his interests in the Parry Sound Colonization Railway with the Ottawa-Arnprior Railway to create the shortest route, via Montreal, to the Atlantic Ocean. Depot Harbour was in business. In 1899, Booth made the new Ottawa-Arnprior-Parry Sound line part of his Canada Atlantic Transit Company, which operated seven ships. In that year, he also bought up another 110 acres (44ha) of land for the Depot Harbour town site which would include 103 family homes, a three-storey, 110-room hotel, a large bunkhouse, a modern school, three churches (Anglican,

Depot Harbour, houses for the management

Presbyterian, and Roman Catholic), two stores, a post office, a butcher shop, and a barber shop. He also added all the services needed for Depot Harbour's transshipping success: a railway station, water tower, and roundhouse, a coal dock, warehouses, two huge freight sheds, and two grain elevators each to hold a million tons of grain and a powerhouse to ensure Depot Harbour had its own supply of electricity.

During the boom years from 1910 to 1928, there was always something going on in Depot Harbour. Fifty to sixty ships would call at Depot Harbour each year, shipping over two million tons of flour, grain, feed, packaged freight, and manufactured goods to eastern and western ports. On any given day, the warehouses were full of spices and silks from the East, wool from Australia, and manufactured goods from Chicago for the Woolworth's five and dime stores. Passenger trains from Ottawa arrived daily.

Depot Harbour's inhabitants were as diverse as the goods flowing in and out. By 1911, there were 650 people living here from English, Irish, French, Italian, German and eleven other European backgrounds. Language barriers were overcome, and the town's social life was harmonious and amicable. By 1926, the population had climbed to 1,600 with as many as 3,000 residents in the summer.

In 1904, Booth sold the Canada Atlantic Transit Railway to the Grand Trunk Railway which, in turn, was amalgamated in 1923 with the Canadian National Railway. This set the stage for Depot Harbour's eventual downfall and its new reputation. No longer would it be the biggest port on the Bay, instead it would be the biggest ghost town.

Depot Harbour was hit by several damaging blows. When the CNR could not afford to mend a vital bridge Depot Harbour lost its role as the shortest route to the Atlantic. In addition the Great Depression destroyed the grain trade and Depot Harbour's massive elevators fell into disuse. With no jobs there was a exodus out of town.

Depot Harbour experienced one more small boom during the Second World War. One of Depot's grain elevators was used to store cordite for the explosives factory at Nobel. The empty elevator caught fire. Flames rushed through, igniting the second elevator loaded with cordite. What happened next was a fireworks show talked about to this day. Some eyewitnesses said the flame was so bright

Depot Harbour, Roman Catholic church

you could read a newspaper at midnight in Parry Sound. Birds died flying into the firelight thinking it was daylight. The heat was so intense that steel melted and train tracks warped as if made of plastic. The dreams and hard work of the people who put Depot Harbour on the map were lost in those ferocious flames.

A coal company tried to operate but closed in 1951. Depot Harobur's status as a Ghost Town was now confirmed. The CNR sold many of the buildings to happy cottagers, who carted them off in pieces for a mere $25. What was left after the scavenging was torn down or left to the elements. A few businesses tried to revitalize the harbour, stockpiling ore and manufacturing fertilizer, but

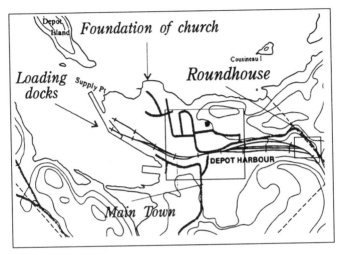

Refer to charts 2202, 2226, 2284

none lasted.

   In 1987, the Ojibwa Indian Band broke the CNR's 99-year lease and regained control of Parry Island. They returned it to its original name, Wasauksing. At present they are working towards self-government. The Ojibwa own all the land around Depot Harbour and permission must be obtained from the Band office before exploring the town.

   If approaching by boat, the first thing you will see are the concrete docks and wharves where ships used to line up three-deep. To the north a forest has now taken root in the remains of the roundhouse, and the concrete company's vault stands empty. As you explore the considerable grid of streets voices call out: neighbours talking over the fence, mothers shouting to their children, people greeting each other in dozens of languages. Or there is the familiar tapping of J.R. Booth's cane on the sidewalk as he strolls through the town, surveying the fruits of his labour and the work of many. The steps that once led up to one of the three churches are still there. Early twentieth-century artifacts lie scattered in dense grass and shrubs, and in the water plenty of broken green Depression glass can be found.

If you are lucky, you may be able to attend one of Dave Thomas's famous slideshows on Depot Harbour's past. Dave is one of the finest "keepers of the past," with an extensive collection of stills and other archival material that keep Depot's memory alive.

Atlantic Wreck

It was November 10, 1903 and the *Atlantic* was riding with a full hold of lumber supplies, twenty-five barrels of coal oil, bailed hay, and other assorted goods, when a crew member heard what he thought was a cannon shot. His ears had picked up what the black night had not yet revealed. An incredible storm was coming their way. When the gale struck, the ship started to take on water. Captain Wright headed the *Atlantic* for Red Rock Lighthouse intending to shelter behind the Pancake Islands. The seasoned crew, trying to hide their mounting panic, watched helplessly as the rush of water surpassed the capacity of the pumps to remove it. Then to their horror a fire exploded out of the right boiler. Most of the twenty-five member crew frantically tried to extinguish the raging flames that were threatening to engulf the 147-foot (44.1-m) steamer. They feared history would repeat itself, for in 1882, the *Atlantic,* then named the *Manitoulin*, had caught fire and tragically taken fifteen lives.

Was she cursed? A giant wave of good luck put the question to rest when it swept aboard and doused the fire. But now a third crisis hit - the *Atlantic* was listing to starboard. The captain managed to navigate her to the sheltering Pancakes and drop anchor. The pumps lowered the water level in the hull and the crew redistributed the cargo to the port side. Soon the anchor was pulled and she was heading back into open water. It was the captain's intention to beach her near Parry Sound and go for assistance. Suddenly, they were faced with a roaring blaze from the hay in the midship gangway. This time it was too much. The alarm was given and the lifeboats launched. One crew member later recalled seeing the cook, R.J. Drinkle, charging toward the waiting lifeboat with some clothing he wanted to save. He tossed the clothing toward the lifeboat where it was snapped up by the wind and sucked into the dark clouds. In Drinkle's panic he jumped into the lifeboat breaking another crewman's leg. The crew and passengers survived, but nothing of the *Atlantic* was saved. The following day, George Stalker, a fisherman at the Minks (see Mink Islands) confirmed a sighting of the charred vessel floating around for some time until it sank where it is today.

The *Atlantic* wreck is some distance west of Parry Sound, near the Spruce Rocks just south of the Spruce

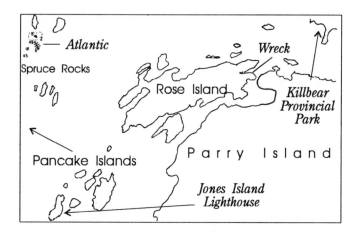

Refer to charts 2202, 2225, 2284

Islands in five to forty feet (1.5 to 12m) of water. There is plenty of "stuff" to make it a interesting dive: her propeller, a tangled chain, machinery, and a smokestack. There is also an engraved brass plaque mounted near the propeller, a memorial to those who lost their lives on the *Manitoulin*. Unfortunately, this site has not been respected by earlier divers; parts of the wreck are covered in graffiti. There is also a snowmobile sitting upright on the bottom near the bow of the wreck. *NOTE: The site is quite open, so be wary of strong westerly winds. Heavy boat traffic is another hazard.*

The salvaging spirit of the neighbourhood is best exemplified by the individual who discovered the name plate for the *Atlantic*: he saw an opportunity that could

The Atlantic, was she cursed?

not to be missed, and made it into an ironing board - currently on display at the West Parry Sound Museum.

Killbear Provincial Park

This, 4,390 acre (1,756ha) natural environment park is ideal for swimming, sunning, fishing, and for the more adventurous, cliff-diving, trail-hiking, and underwater diving. There are seven campgrounds within the park, with a total of 883 campsites. A dive site at Harold Point offers dramatic underwater scenery: boulders, cliffs, ledges, and curious fish. The depth ranges from 40 to 90 feet (12 to

27m).

The area was once an important native hunting ground. The Nipissing Indians hunted here until the 1640s when the Iroquois took over the territory. In turn, the Iroquois were replaced by the Ojibwa in the 1750s, who hunted here until the 1850s. The first white settler, Matthew Scott, arrived in 1855, and for the next fifty years the area was known for hemlock harvesting, a lumber mill, and a sugar bush operation. Not until the late 1950s did activity slow down, leaving the area to enjoy a comfortable retirement as a provincial park.

Jones Island Lighthouse

Every lighthouse keeper had to struggle to avert boredom. The keeper on Jones Island, however, didn't have the opportunity to be bored - he was too busy dodging all those bees. Imported from the Holy Land by the island's owner, B.F. Jones, the bees made quite a hobby. Mr. Jones lost the distinction of owning the most unusual pet on the Bay only recently, as there is an island in the Sans Souci area that is home to two llamas.

Jane McLeod Wreck

Island living, especially in frosty November, was getting a little stale for Captain Robinson and the crew of the *Jane McLeod*. About as stale as the food they were eating. They had been stranded on this miserable island, now called

McLeod Island, for five days, living on what they had managed to salvage from their schooner, which recently ran
aground on the island's shore. The men were expecting to
see help soon as a vessel does not disappear on the Bay for
five days without someone asking questions - they hoped.
The captain was working hard to keep their spirits up,
which was difficult with Ed, one of crew, so diligently carv-
ing out his headstone. One wonders if the captain ever
mentioned to Ed that he had spelled the word schooner
incorrectly?

Their trouble began on November 4, 1890. After
dropping off a load of hay and oats at Parry Sound they
anchored near the island for the night. The ship parted

Jones Island Lighthouse

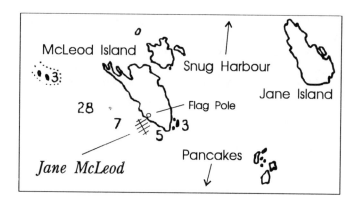

Refer to charts 2203, 2225, 2284

from her anchor chain, and the heavy winds ran her aground. The crew were rescued but not the poor *Jane McLeod*. Successive winters were not kind to her. Battered regularly by heavy rain, ice, and snowstorms, she finally snapped apart like a twig before she could be salvaged.

The *Jane McLeod* is an interesting dive. She lies less than 100 feet (30m) from the south shore of the island, and even though the weather has had its way with her, you can still tell she's a schooner. Bits and pieces of her deck and rigging are scattered about the site. Her bow is in twenty feet (6m) and her stern is in 25 feet (7.5m) of water. *NOTE: Westerly winds can get very strong very quickly. As McLeod Island is privately owned do not go ashore while anchored at the site.*

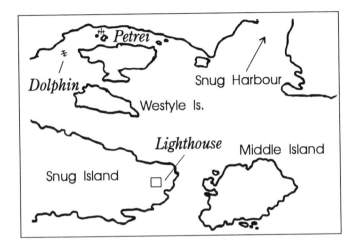

Refer to chart 2203, sheet 1

As for Ed's tombstone, it was salvaged by a cottager who used it for part of his deck. Recently donated to the West Parry Sound Museum, it can be seen together with the *Atlantic* name plate ironing board (p116).

Dolphin and Petrie
Snug Harbour

While in the area, you may want to dive on the wrecks around Snug Harbour — a cottage settlement with a government dock and small boat marina. Lying in a calm backwater to the northwest of Snug Harbour, between

Red Rock Lighthouse

the mainland and the northern tip of the small unnamed island to the east of Westyle Island, is a 49-foot (14.7m) steam tug locally known as the *Dolphin*. Island lore has it that the *Dolphin* was built in 1900 and was owned by Midland lumber baron, James Playfair (see p. 5). The wreck was blown up by cottagers to discourage divers and is now of minimal interest. What remains rests on a silt bottom in about 20 feet (6m) of water. Unlike many of the other wrecks, it is accessible in all kinds of weather, is easy to find, and easy to dive on.

In a channel to the east rests the *Petrie* wreck, a small fishing boat which shelters much marine life. *NOTE: Please respect the cottagers near this dive site or it may fall to the same explosive fate as the Dolphin.*

Red Rock Lighthouse

This unusually shaped lighthouse which appears to be more barrel-shaped than its traditional tower-shaped mates, has safely guided ships from the open water to Parry Sound for decades. The stout body of the Red Rock Light takes up most of the island, and perhaps this is why its deceased lightkeeper, Adam Brown, is still a local legend. With sound mind he managed to tend this lonely, claustrophobic place for forty years. The light keepers and their families' names are carved into the rock.

Red Rock has seen its fair share of storms, and has probably lost more to the Bay than any other light. A wooden predecessor was called Tower Rock Lighthouse and it stood on the southernmost island of the Mink Islands, now called Old Tower Island. Georgian Bay gave a grace period of a year, before sweeping the light away in the winter of 1879. The second structure, also of wood, followed its sibling into the dark depths of the Bay. The third (and one would hope final) light seen today has a metal base and is cemented in place. The lamp from the 1879 light can be viewed at the West Parry Sound Museum.

The Mink Islands

"It wasn't what you'd call pleasure the way we fished up there in the fall in open tugs. We took every day that came along.... We fished 7 days a week...20 hours a day. Three months and you'd never miss a day.... Not like these bankers – I call them bankers [because they keep banker's hours]," said Charlie Parr, comparing his life as a Minks fisherman to the fishermen of today.

From the early 1880s to the mid-1930s, the Minks were the site of one of the busiest fishing stations on the Bay. The work was hard and the hours long; up to 20 hours a day not only catching the fish but freighting it as well. According to Charlie Parr: "we'd get off the lake at 5:00 at night. The tug would only run 8 miles an hour, a steam tug, a 3 hour run [to Parry Sound.] And we had 150 boxes of fish to unload there and then we'd have to load coal and then get back out to the Minks to go on the lake at 6:00 a.m.. Twice a week we did that. We'd only get an hour of sleep or so. And we used to hope and pray that we could get into town on Saturday to do a little shopping

Family on the Mink Islands

Pulling up the nets

and we'd hope for maybe 1,500 [pounds] of fish. But we'd get 2,200 or 2,500 [pounds]. And us already with 2 day's shipping to do. We'd just throw them aboard and weigh them on the way in.... Truckloads of fish used to go out."

The Parr family has been in the fishing business for over 90 years. Charlie started fishing at the Umbrellas (see page 100) in the 1920s and moved over to the Minks in 1930. At this time Charlie estimated there were about 105 residents on the windswept islands. The nets in the 1800s were tended from small mackinaw sailing boats and so the fishermen took up summer residence close to their fishing grounds. The Minks offered everything the families needed: ice houses, net houses, warehouses, a small church, and wooden shanties. A lone cow provided milk for the children and much later a floating grocery store visited twice a week.

A diary written in 1896 by a traveler named Cleveland Hamilton paints a picturesque portrait of early Minks life. During the evenings the families shared large dinners with plenty of food. Afterwards, a visiting fiddler stirred up the eager crowd. Children dozed in the arms of their smiling mothers, and the rugged features on the men relaxed, eased by the reels and jigs that spun through the air. "Shoes not the lightest, beat the floor, not the smoothest" well into the wee hours. Outside, the cobalt canopy of a Georgian Bay summer night overwhelmed him, "Orion was in the east and the northern lights flickered and danced in the northwest." The native translation for northern lights is "the dead are dancing" - perhaps this is where the spirits of the Mink's people can be found?

By the late 1940s, the Minks fishing stations were no more. Faster boats, changing marketing patterns, and most significantly, extremely low fish stocks could no longer support the same number of men. All that remains of one of the biggest operations on the Bay is a few crumbling shacks and a bit of debris scattered along the shores. Most of the islands are owned by cottagers. One family has converted the net house into a summer home. Stalker Island is private but from the water, you can see one of the early shanties now dilapidated. Perhaps this was the one Cleveland Hamilton wrote about. Buildings which were once part of the fishing camp on Boucher Island have been renovated into private cottages. Burned debris and bits of coloured glass are the only hints of a past life on

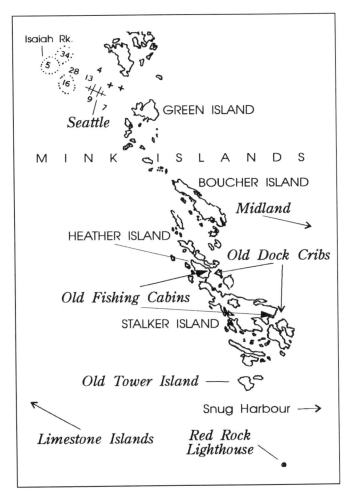

Refer to charts 2225, 2243, 2284

Heather Island. North of Heather Island the large ice-house still stands on the barren rock. At one time it was filled with ice cut from the Bay in March ready for the long summer ahead. The quaint shack on Pine Island is a later building. According to Glen Parr (who still fishes the Bay), this was someones honeymoon shack.

The most interesting relics from the early fishing days are below water. The area is full of "valuable junk", old bottles, boots, shoes, tools, plates, bottles, chamber pots and anything else that may have fallen from the boats during loading and unloading. These mementos belong to the Minks. Please leave them there for generations to come. As well, there are two wrecks in this area (see below). *NOTE: Heather and Stalker Islands are privately owned.*

Whether the history of the fishing stations intrigue you or not, the Mink Islands are definitely worth a visit - they remain one of our favorite spots. Walking barefoot on their ancient pink granite, worn smooth by the ice age and centuries of waves, is a unique experience. This remote collection of islands offers shelter from the wind, and some of the best sunsets on the Bay.

Midland Wreck

The *Midland* is a great wreck to dive on. The only problem is finding it. This 62-foot (18.6-m) tug, built in Midland by Robert J. Morril in 1896 and launched as the *D.L. White*, supposedly foundered off a shoal on the northeast corner of Green Island in 1923. According to those who have dived on it, she can be found curved into the clay bottom in about 50 feet (15m) of clear water, just southeast of the Minks. Her stern is intact, and plenty of machinery, as well as her propeller and rudder, are visible. We spent two fruitless hours trying to find the *Midland*. Before setting out to find this wreck, consult dive charts and ask a few locals at the docks in Snug Harbour.

Seattle Wreck

Although the ship may be long forgotten by many, the *Seattle* is immortalized in this area. On November 11, 1903, during the same gale that fanned the fires of the *Atlantic* (p 116), this 160-foot (48-m) steamer's engines failed about 40 miles (64km) out of Parry Sound. The wind and waves crashed her into the Minks, angrily grinding her hull along the ledges of Green Island. She had served eleven years on the Great Lakes and, even though she was sinking, others had plans for her to serve many more. The following summer, word spread among the Snug Harbour cottagers that a steamer had sunk during the winter with cargo intact: a load of prime lumber slated for delivery to Detroit. The quick-thinking group promptly went out to the wreck and salvaged as much lumber as they could. Considering the number of cottages around Snug Harbour and the old Adanac Hotel on Franklin Island that are said to be built with this wood, their efforts were extremely successful.

Like the *Midland*, the *Seattle* can be a difficult site to find. But we did - after six hours and a lot of chart consulting. The fairly intact wreck is located well offshore west of Green Island in about 20 to 25 feet (6 to 7.5m) of water. On calm days, the *Seattle*'s boilers are just visible from the surface.

NOTE: We do not recommend diving on it, or even looking for it, when the wind is strong and westerly because of its proximity to rocks.

The Limestone Islands

From a distance, the Limestones appear as a white mirage over the water, their sparse trees barely breaking the horizon. What could they possibly offer? To say the least, the Limestones are humble and unassuming, but within ten minutes on their ivory shores, they reveal a treasure trove of history. There are no traces of fishing stations or lumber mills here – no, the early nineteenth century is far too recent for the Limestones. Try going back some 450 million years to a time when the continental plates were shifting, and the Limestone Islands were actually the bottom of a shallow tropical sea close to the equator. Over the millennia, the earth moved, glaciers melted, and these islands made their way north to Georgian Bay, bringing with them a permanent record of prehistory in the form of countless fossils. The Limestone Islands were one of the highlights of our trip. Take your time here - the more you look, the more the island will reveal.

The scent of chamomile is strong as you land on the South Limestone Island. There are a few low shrubs, trees and grasses which provide nesting areas for the gulls and terns, but it is underfoot where the Island's history unfolds. The South Limestone Island, in particular, is covered with fossils of all kinds — clams, coral, worms, shell beds, twigs, leaves, bone fragments, and much more. The long worm-like fossils are the segmented shells of the cephalopod — a tentacled squid-like creature that used its shell as a flotation device. Some cephalopods grew up to

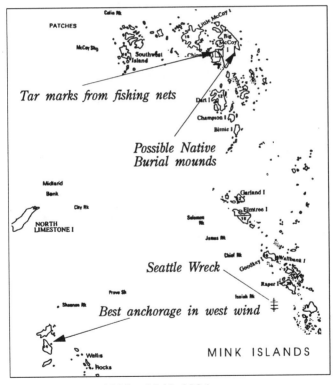

Refer to charts 2225,   2243, 2284

six feet (1.8m) long (one fisherman reported he saw fossils this large on Manitoulin Island), all were carnivores and may have lived together in schools. Some of the other coiled fossils are prehistoric coral. The smaller shells are those of the brachiopods – early versions of bi-valued clams. It is easy to become lost in another world on the Limestones. As one old-time fisherman put it, it is a land of "big alligators and snakes and big footprints." There's plenty for snorkelers and divers to investigate underwater as well. Many unique fossils can be found in the rock formations on the southern tip of the South Limestone Island in no more than ten feet (3m) of water. *NOTE: Take a camera in order to record any "finds," as it is against the law to remove anything from the Limestones.* They are protected by the Ministry of Natural Resources. Remember, you're traipsing on 450 million years of nature's work. It may be difficult to anchor close to the Limestones because of their smooth rock bottom. Anchor off shore and use a dinghy. The best place is off of a bay on the eastern shore of the South Limestone Island. We recommend nosing your way into it.

The Ghost of McCoy
The McCoy Islands

There are two moons tonight. The full silver body in the sky and its shimmering companion reflected in the dark waters below. All is still until a long, low, mournful howl escapes from the deepest part of Big McCoy Island's woods. A ripple in the water traces its path as it echoes and bounces against the smaller surrounding islands. Hairs rise on the backs of any living creatures in the vicinity. They hold their collective breath, waiting for the second chilling howl to signal the end to yet another yearly vocalization by the ghost of Mr. McCoy.

Legend has it that at the full moon in the month of September, the ghost of Mr. McCoy lets out two terrible screams to protest his murder. History provides little sympathy for Mr. McCoy's untimely demise, as he was the 'ly'n, cheat'n, thieve'n' type. He set up shop on the island to trade with the local natives - and bragged quite openly about cheating them. His own ignorance, however, cost him his life. One quiet September evening, with a full moon providing plenty of light, someone set out to punish Mr. McCoy for his dishonesty. A silhouetted figure swooped down on his shack and justice was meted out. Mr. McCoy traded no more.

John Hillis, a former fisherman on the Bay, remembers as a boy hearing firsthand about the McCoy ghost. Bill Sing, a local scoundrel, had spent the night alone on the island while passing through the area. That night Bill was ripped from his slumber by a low wretched scream. Terrified, he got off the island as fast as he could. Now if you go to the McCoys, you'll realize one has to be pretty scared to dare the surrounding waters by night - full September moon or not - as this is one of the most treacherous and shoal infested areas on the Bay. Back in town, Bill was frightened enough to publicly vow never to set foot on the McCoys again. And he never did.

Some still believe in the legend. Every September a

handful of people go out to the island to wait for McCoy's pleas of innocence.

At any time the McCoys can be rather spooky. They are a remote collection of islands ringed by shoals. There appears to have been a small fishing operation on Big McCoy. On the west side the crisscross tar imprints of their linen nets can still be seen on the rocks. An even more mysterious find is tucked into a small bay on the east side of the island. We passed this treasure a number of times, noticing nothing but feeling uncomfortable. Then we realized what we weren't seeing. We were standing on a huge, perfect mound of rocks 35x60 feet (10.5x18m) in diameter which locals believe is an ancient burial mound. We tried but we could find no information about these lichen-covered rocks. An expert at the Royal Ontario Museum said that if it is a mound it could date back thousands of years. No artifacts remain as the acidity of the area would have long dissolved the buried contents.

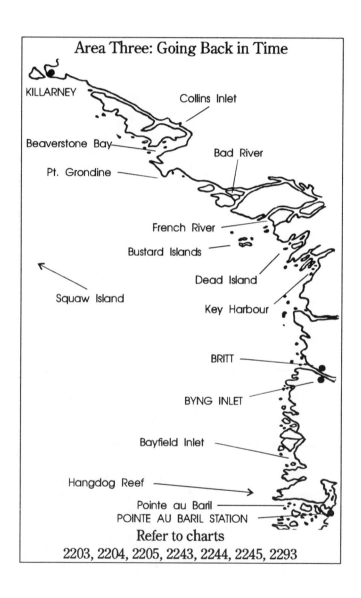

Area Three: Going Back in Time

KILLARNEY

Collins Inlet

Beaverstone Bay

Pt. Grondine

Bad River

French River

Bustard Islands

Dead Island

Squaw Island

Key Harbour

BRITT

BYNG INLET

Bayfield Inlet

Hangdog Reef

Pointe au Baril
POINTE AU BARIL STATION

Refer to charts
2203, 2204, 2205, 2243, 2244, 2245, 2293

3

Reaching Back in Time : The North Shore

Prehistoric... frozen in time... ancient, silent mountains rising from the deep green-blue water; islands worn smooth by hundreds of thousands of years of waves licking at their shores; generations of Algokians telling and retelling their legends.... These are the things that come to mind when trying to describe the heavy atmosphere of the Bay's northern shores. It hits you out in the open water, in Beaverstone Bay, on the Hangdog Bank, and off the Killarney shores, and it's as if you've entered another world, another time.

This area, now seemingly untouched, was once a booming industrial centre: lumber mills, fishing stations, mining towns dotted its shores. Raw materials were processed and sold. The air was thick with smoke, the water choked with logs, and the fish, "stacked up like cordwood" on the docks. Profiteers walked a thin line between progress and outright pillaging.

A feverish burst of activity, but you'd hardly know it today. For the Bay is a patient teacher. While we were furiously stripping her of her trees, and rock, and fish, she waited. When the sawdust choked spawning sites and the lumber supply dwindled and the demand for coal lessened and the railway routes were canceled, she waited. When everyone left, she remained, quietly reclaiming what was hers, reclaiming what we had abandoned, and healing her scars. But she did leave remnants of our past, being the kind teacher that she is; a few foundations and decaying docks as clues....

The Asia Mystery

It was a few days after the big hurricane of September 14, 1882, and Georgian Bay had regained her calm demeanor. The water was tranquil, practically inviting, and the skies were a vibrant blue. On his way north up the Bay's eastern coast Captain A.M. McGregor spotted something unusual on the shoreline of the Limestone Islands (see area two). His discoveries were most distressing: a large steamer trunk, a door, and a pillow slip with the name of the steamer, the *Asia*, embroidered on it. Something was terribly wrong.

The *Asia*, a 136-foot (40.8-m) passenger and freight steamer, had been an old canaller — short, stubby, and top heavy. Built in 1873 in St. Catharines, this nine-year-old workhorse was part of the Beatty line, and at the time

The Asia, Georgian Bay's worst ship disaster

chartered to the Great Northern Transit Company. At first she was mostly used to transport cargo to the CPR construction crews on Lake Superior, but was quickly "promoted" into passenger service. Competition was strong among the transit lines which exerted heavy pressure on their captains to deliver as much cargo as fast as possible.

On the afternoon of September 14th, Christy Anne Morrison manoeuvered up the crowded gangway of the *Asia*. She was relieved to have made it on board as she had already missed the *Northern Belle* and would now be late in meeting her Aunt. On her way to her berth she ran into her cousin the first mate. She put her bags in her room and watched the stream of passengers, many dressed in their finest, make their way through the ship chatting and laughing. Many of the twenty-five member crew were struggling against the blustery wind to load cargo and cattle. At midnight the gangways were closed and the *Asia* left Owen Sound, loaded to the rafters and beyond with logging equipment, provisions, horses and other livestock, a team of loggers, and 122 passengers and crew. Late passengers had to scramble for space and many ended up sleeping in the hallways, in cargo holds, and even on deck with the overflow cargo. During an hour stop at Presqu'ile (see story chapter four) deckhands leaned into the wind as they passed cordwood hand to hand into the steamer. No one seemed concerned about the storm warning that had been issued.

Christy Ann became frightened as the vessel began to roll. She dressed and made her way through the ship, one hand against the wall to steady herself. It was then that she witnessed the crew tossing cargo and pushing terrified animals overboard into the huge white crested waves that leapt up at the ship rails. She ran back and locked herself in her room, the sound of the shrieking horses still ringing in her ears. Little did she know the horror was just beginning.

After a night of fitful sleep, another passenger, Dunkan Tinkiss and his uncle rose for breakfast. There was a heavy quiet about the room. The ship had been sailing in the lee of the Bruce but the captain knew that when he hit the open, he would meet winds that had the full rage of Lake Huron behind them. But he had a schedule to keep, and was determined to hold course. By nine a.m.

the ship was in danger. The *Asia* rolled and listed in the huge troughs. The intense wind split the crests off waves and spewed them over the creaking and moaning vessel. The pounding and heaving and churning continued for hours; people were seasick and exhausted, crying and shrieking with each wave that swept over the steamer.

By eleven a.m., the *Asia* was in a hurricane, and there was little Captain Savage could do. Below deck, chairs, tables, dishes, boxes of cargo, and anything else not nailed down crashed from side to side. In a final attempt to save the ship, Captain Savage veered westward towards Lonely Island. This manoeuver did her in. The *Asia* vanished between two monster waves and slowly rolled over. Dunkan's uncle grabbed his nephew, shouting, "Jump up Dunk the boat is doomed." The two pushed their way through the hysterical crowd. The ship had righted itself, then was struck by another massive blow. As she rolled over Dunkan and his Uncle with others scrambled up her side onto the hurricane deck. Her stern nosed into the water. The Bay was swallowing her up. Passengers jumped into the cold turbulent waters, grabbing desperately at the scattered cargo. Dunkan called for his uncle to jump then dove in and swam toward the lifeboat. He was lifted by a giant wave and when he was slammed back down the life boat was overturned and sinking. Dunkan searched frantically for his Uncle but he was gone. Drowning people were desperately grabbing at him, and pulling him under the churning waves.

Christy Anne climbed over the rail and was flung into the water by the force of the hurricane. A lifeboat with her cousin and other men came towards her. As she was pulled in, another hand reached up from the water. It was Dunkan, pleading with them to take him aboard. Secure in the lifeboat Dunkan looked back at the *Asia,* a sight he could never forget: "a struggling mass of humanity... clinging to pieces of timber and other wreckage to prolong their lives even for a few seconds." Another wave hit, effortlessly flipping over the lifeboat and its 18 passengers. Christy Ann surfaced but noticed many did not. The survivors clung onto the boat gunnels, bracing as each wave flung over them. Those suffering from injury or exposure were washed away, others just gave up and disappeared into the black.

Eventually the waves subsided, and they were able to right the lifeboat. Besides the two teenagers, Christy Ann and Dunkan, there were two loggers, Mr. Little, the purser, the second mate, the Captain, and Christy Anne's cousin. The lifeboat drifted aimlessly, its silent passengers shivering and trembling. Day turned into night. Christy Anne stared out at the waves that seethed relentlessly around the lifeboat like sinister black oil. Suddenly the captain caught sight of a blinking light from a distant lighthouse. They began to sing, their voices weak and hoarse but full of hope. They all stared at the rhythmic pulse of light for what seemed hours. When the wind shifted and the boat began to drift in the opposite direction, no one uttered a word. The despair was too great.

The two lumbermen were the first to die. Christy Anne, feeling the others drifting away, began to sing again. Mr. Little stared at her, murmured the words to 'Sweet by and By,' then quietly died. Christy Anne held her cousin's head in her arms, his lips were blue and his skin translucent from the cold. He too drifted away. When the sun rose the waters were still churning. Dunkan didn't move his gaze from the Captain's face. He had been lucid just a few hours ago but now he seemed to be drifting in and out of fitful sleep. The Captain stopped moving. Dunkan began shaking him frantically, "Yes, yes I'll be up in a minute," muttered the delirious captain. A wave hit the side of the boat and Dunkan was thrown against the bodies. When he sat up the captain was dead. Now it was just Christy Anne and Dunkan and their grisly cargo. All that day they drifted towards the mainland, and landed near what is thought to be Byng Inlet. The two teenagers dragged the boat ashore, removed the bodies, and set back out, aiming to reach a lighthouse they had spotted a few miles away. With only a branch for a paddle, the two did not get far. Drained of all energy, they went ashore and fell asleep on the beach. The next morning they tried again to reach the lighthouse, only to find it was an abandoned derrick.

About to give up all hope, they spotted two people - an Ojibwa couple coming towards them in a canoe. Three days had passed from the time the *Asia* had gone down before the two seventeen year olds made there way into Parry Sound in the couple's tiny sailboat. There they learned the terrible news - of the 122 passengers they were the only survivors.

Speculation was rife: the *Asia* went down about 35 miles (56km) northwest of Parry Sound and probably ten miles (16 km) from French River; the Asia foundered off the Limestones not any farther north than Byng Inlet; the *Asia* hit a dangerous shoal about twelve miles (19km) off

Christy Anne Morrison

the Blackbill Islands and had run aground on an unmarked reef... we still don't know. At an official inquiry into the loss of the *Asia*, it was determined she was ill-equipped for service on the Bay and was particularly ill-prepared for the hurricane of September 14, as she was top heavy with cargo and carrying too many passengers. The inquiry suggested the presence of some unmarked shoals may have contributed to her foundering. Although later disproved, the loss of the *Asia* prompted the government to further chart these deceptive waters.

The story of the *Asia* and its two brave survivors is perhaps Georgian Bay's best known tale. Many hours have been spent poring over maps, navigational charts, and news clippings, and exploring the Bay's waters in an effort to locate the wreck. It is rumoured that one man even waited for the same weather and wind conditions, then set himself afloat in a lifeboat, hoping to get an indication from that of the location of the elusive ship. As for Christy Anne and Dunkan, they did meet once later in life, and it is reported that neither spoke a word about the tragic events of that September of 1882.

Turtle Rock
Shawanaga Bay

The young Ojibwa boy could see the heavy grey clouds moving in from the open waters. The wind was picking up and the water was getting choppy. He had to get his canoe safely to shore. It got darker and colder and soon the waves were propelling him towards the rocks. He paddled furiously away from the danger, but the wind and waves whipped his canoe around, as if to show him his fate. Suddenly in the glistening spray, the brave saw a huge turtle. Taking it as a sign, he prayed to the giant turtle for good weather to bring him home safely. The waves and wind subsided, the clouds opened up and the sun came beating down on the young man's face. He turned to thank the creature and saw not a giant live turtle but one made of rock and sitting securely on the jagged shore. He fell to his knees, thanking the turtle and leaving an offering

Natives in European Dress

of deer meat. Over many years other travelers in the area would leave offerings of tobacco, food, and beads with the turtle to ensure calm weather. The peculiarly shaped rock and its power to control the wind was even mentioned in Anna B. Jameson's 1834 travel journal, *Winter Studies and Summer Rambles in Canada* (see Anna Jameson.)

Travel northeast of the Twin Sister Islands along the mainland until the distinct form of a turtle's head and body can be seen. Turtle Rock is an important spiritual place to the people from the Shawanaga Reserve and they ask that it be treated with respect.

Metamora Wreck

If the *Metamora* could have rewritten history and chosen her fate, she may very well have preferred to go down in a blaze of glory, shooting her cannon at the Irish national terrorists, the Fenians, as they invaded Canada from south of the border in the late 1860s. It sure sounds a lot better than what really happened.

The *Metamora* led many lives in her forty years of service on the Bay. Built in 1864 in Cleveland, the 115-foot (34.5-m) wooden tug was sold north of the border for use on the Great Lakes. During the Fenian scare, the government converted her into a gunboat, complete with a cannon and armour plating, to patrol and protect the Lakes. When the Fenian threat dissipated in the early 1870s, her armour plating and cannon were removed and the ship returned to civilian service. She returned to Georgian Bay as a passenger and freight boat. She did this contentedly for almost thirty-five years.

On July 30, 1907, the *Metamora* left Midland for Byng Inlet. When approaching the east end of Nadeau Island she caught fire in Shawanaga Inlet. Her crew escaped to the nearby island, leaving the *Metamora* to burn to the waterline. No cannons, no applause, no victory band.

Her wreck, too, is without glory. Lying in 5 to 15 feet (1.5 to 4.5m) of water, the *Metamora* is easy to spot because of the navigational day marker attached to her boiler, which is partially above water. Because of the fire, her stern is the only largely intact segment with her rudder, steam engine, propeller, and boiler all in place.

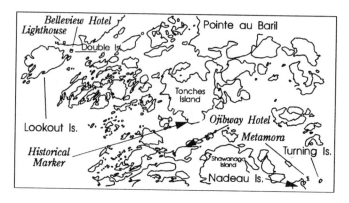

Refer to charts 2203, 2243

Pointe au Baril Ghost Town
Pointe au Baril Station

The voyageur thought it was exhaustion tricking his eyes
when he saw the wet glistening barrel bob merrily past
Double Island. He held it over his head, water dripping
down on his face, so that his partners could read the sten-
cil on the barrel: WHISKY. They started a fire, cooked dinner, and set about emptying the barrel, all the while toast-
ing their *bonne chance*. In the morning, after a good
"heavy sleep", the men packed up. Before leaving, they set
the empty barrel upside down on a pole. So marked, this
point became known as Pointe au Baril by all the traders
who travelled by thereafter. One local claimed it could still
be seen in the 1870s. Someone else cut off one side of
the barrel and placed a lantern inside it, creating the first

unofficial lighthouse on the point.

The first official lighthouse was constructed in 1889, and was manned by light keeper and soon-to-be entrepreneur, Samuel Oldfield. Oldfield ran the lighthouse between 1889 and 1907, but soon began juggling other careers: postmaster in 1892, and local "resort tycoon" in 1900, when he built and operated the two-story Belleview Hotel and its surrounding cottages on Lookout Island. The original hotel was built of wood salvaged from a wrecked lumber carrier in the area. Destroyed by fire in 1920, it was rebuilt as a hunting and fishing resort. It could house from twenty-five to thirty guests, as well as three to four families in its surrounding cottages. Very little is known about the Belleview and its demise. One woman remembered in the 1950s being there with her parents for

The Belleview. Haunted?

a week while their cruiser was repaired. She described it as being in its "twilight years." The dock was unsafe, the rooms, dark and musty. She stopped in the middle of her story, finally adding that she had had a very "unsettling" experience near the Belleview piano. It was late afternoon and she was sure that she had seen a figure move through the room. She looked again but it was gone. Spooked, she did not leave her mother's side for the rest of the stay. Forty years later, the woman remains convinced she saw a ghost that day.

Whatever the truth, the end results couldn't be better for ghost town enthusiasts. Entering the inlet, the lighthouse can be spotted on the northwest corner of the mainland. Across from it is Lookout Island; and suddenly, you are back in time. This is an amazingly atmospheric site, as the now dilapidated Belleview Hotel, its boathouse, icehouse, and surrounding cottages are still standing. From your boat (and we suggest you stay on your boat and heed the "No Trespassing" signs,) the feeling of history, of a once-spirited resort, wraps you in its magic.

On the mainland, just east of the lighthouse (which was automated in 1983), there is a rundown shack and a few old rusty rings in the rocks. Early photographs reveal that there was once a substantial dock, possibly the place where tugs picked up the produce from the fish-packing facility.

Across from the Champlain monument on Ojibway Island another delight awaits. The grand old Ojibway Hotel, with its three-stories and sweeping porch, was built in 1903 by Hamilton Davis, a native of Rochester, New

York. When he added two stores, a post office, a boat repair facility, and a dance pavilion, the Ojibway clinched its position as the social hub. In fact, it maintained its role in the community much longer than did the hotels out on the open. When it started to lose money, the local cottagers couldn't bear to see it meet the fate of the more humble Belleview so they purchased it in 1964. To this day, it is their not-for-profit club.

The village of Pointe Au Baril Station is located at the end of the inlet. In 1906, the CPR extended a line making Pointe au Baril yet another important transshipment point on the Bay. Today, it is the main service centre for the cottagers and resorts in this area. Along this inlet is the entrance to Sturgeon Bay Provincial Park, where there is a dock, launching ramps, and camping facilities.

Bayfield Inlet

It's only fitting that we devote some space to this namesake inlet to commemorate the man who devoted forty years to surveying the Great Lakes, four of which were spent charting and naming Georgian Bay's tens of thousands of islands and shoals. Henry Wolsey Bayfield became a British Navy man in 1806 at the ripe old age of eleven. By 1815 he was a lieutenant, well on his way to becoming a disciplined and meticulous surveyor. So much so that when Captain William Fitzwilliam Owen was sent from England to do a survey of the Great Lakes in 1816, he recruited the twenty-year-old Bayfield. Bayfield's work was so precise that he was quickly promoted to Admiralty

Lt. Henry Wolsey Bayfield

Surveyor and eventually took over from Owen. Between 1819 and 1822 Bayfield surveyed the Bay with the help of a few assistants — including Asher Mundy's son Israel (see story page 2). He went on to survey all of the Great Lakes, the St. Lawrence River, the Gulf of St. Lawrence, Northumberland Strait, Cape Breton Island, and Labrador, and was promoted twice; Rear Admiral in 1856 and full Admiral in 1867.

And he deserved it all, as surveying in those days was difficult, to say the least. The surveying crew crammed into two six-oared rowboats, with enough provisions to last six weeks. But he seemed to take the unpleasant aspects of his job - and the weather - in stride. Bayfield described the conditions years later, "I slept in all weathers in the Boat, or on the shore upon a Buffaloe robe under the Boat's mainsail thrown over a few branches placed on the ground. Many a night Have I slept, in this way, when the Thermometer was down near Zero, and sometimes even below it. Yet even this was not so wearing as trying to sleep, in vain, in the warm nights of summer... in the smoke of a fire to keep off the clouds of Moschettoes which literally darkened the air."

They surveyed so many islands, it is not surprising that Bayfield ran out of the names of royalty and well-respected officers and had to resort to naming islands after lower classes of soldiers and sailors as well as relatives, friends, girlfriends, ships, shapes, and current events.

Although Bayfield contributed greatly to the hydrography of the Bay, the one thing he was unable to do was accurately sound the depths of the waters. The loss of the *Asia* in 1882 prompted further surveying of the Bay, and in August 1883, Captain John Boulton, in his 120-foot (36-m) wooden tug the Bayfield, began a ten-year sounding of the waters. With a few amendments, some of Boulton's charts are still in use on the Bay today.

Byng Inlet
Britt

14th March 1755; 11:58 a.m.. A handful of men stand on the deck of the *Monarch*, one is blindfolded. At high noon, British Rear Admiral John Byng is to be executed. His crime: neglect of duty in battle. Technically, he is

Byng Inlet, 1895

guilty but he is also the scapegoat the British government needs to deflect an onslaught of political protest. Ethically, he is an innocent man.

Two years earlier, at the beginning of the Seven Years' War between Britain and France, Byng and his troops were sent to help secure Minorca, a Mediterranean island base, from a potential takeover by the French. They arrived to find the French virtually in command. Seeing the hopelessness of the situation and wanting to avoid unnecessary loss of life Byng pulled his men out and returned to Britian. The government did not see it that way, however. Needing someone to blame for the fall of Minorca they singled out Byng and charged him with cowardice, disaffection, and neglect of duty in battle. He was acquitted of the first two charges, but not the third and was sentenced to death. The clock struck twelve noon, and in a matter of seconds, Rear Admiral Byng was dead, a bullet to the head. His story was over. Over half-a-century later, surveyor Admiral Henry Wolsey Bayfield, in a gesture of respect, immortalized Byng by naming a Canadian inlet after the proud soldier who, in the end, gave up his own life for the lives of his men.

The town of Byng Inlet was blessed with a natural harbour and a huge supply of superior timber, making it a very profitable centre. In 1902, the Holland and Graves Lumber Company built what would become the second largest sawmill in Canada at this site, complete with lumber yard, planing mill, numberless shanties and houses, and one big boarding house. Soon there were stores, three churches, a hotel, a dance hall, and a movie house to keep the residents entertained. On an average day in 1910, the mill shipped by rail via Britt no fewer than fifteen box cars loaded with 20,000 board feet of lumber. It was a case of too much, too fast, too soon. By 1927 with the timber supply exhausted, the mill shut down. Byng residents left in droves, abandoning their homes to the elements or the scavengers, whichever came first.

As the town of Byng Inlet declined, its northerly neighbour, the town of Britt, thrived. In 1866, a man by the name of Gibson came to the inlet and built a sawmill on Old Mill Island. His workers erected homes on the mainland north of the island. They called their community Byng Inlet North. In 1880, a larger mill opened farther east, and they both continued to operate for the next

Captain Black Pete Campbell

eleven years, until a fire almost flattened both villages. Byng Inlet North did not bounce back quickly; it was on the verge of becoming a ghost town. In 1908, the railway saved the day, as the CPR built a coal dock on the north shore near the Still River to service its northern posts. The area, now named Dunlop after the resident engineer, was back in business. In 1927, a post office was built and the town was renamed Britt (after a CPR fuel superintendent.) Today Britt is a key oil port on the Bay: in by tanker, out by rail. There is little left to see of the past in Byng Inlet. A few old stores and houses found on the first street back from the shore road can be seen from the water, as well as the original church and hotel.

The Northern Belle

Northern Belle Wreck

When Captain Black Pete Campbell decided to do something, he did it very well. After years of employment with the Beatty family as the reliable and resourceful captain of their steamer, the *Waubuno*, (see story in chapter two) Black Pete set out on his own to take advantage of the now booming local passenger and freight service in the Bay. In 1876, he formed the Georgian Bay Navigation Company with other interested parties. Their first purchase was a recently built American steamer, the *Gladys*, renamed the

Northern Belle. She was immediately put into local service, leaving Collingwood to visit ports from Owen Sound to Sault Ste. Marie - in direct competition with Black Pete's former vessel, the Beatty-owned *Waubuno*. But Black Pete and the Beattys had an amenable relationship, and soon the Beattys bought into Black Pete's company, now owning two of the best known and most popular passenger and freight steamers on the Bay.

The *Northern Belle* served a successful twenty years on the Bay, shuttling thousands of tourists, fishermen, lumber men, and homesteaders - until November 7, 1898. She was moored at Byng Inlet, safe from the open waters but not safe from fire. She burned quickly and sank into the dark waters of the inlet. Nothing could be salvaged, her career was over.

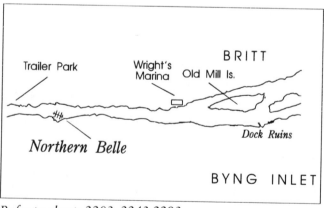

Refer to charts 2203, 2243, 2293

Her popularity as a dive site is almost comparable to her above-water reputation. And she is easy to find. Visible just beneath the surface of the water, she is resting just west of Old Mill Island, against the southern shore of the inlet, in less than 10 feet (3m) of water. This 129-foot (38.7-m) wreck is fairly intact with bits of debris scattered along her hull. At present visibility is good, but reeds threaten to take over the site. The *Northern Belle* is a good site for both diver and snorkeller.

NOTE: The only hazards are a sometimes strong current and boating traffic in the inlet.

Key Harbour

As the only town on the Bay whose livelihood was derived from iron ore, Key Harbour was known as the "Pittsburgh of Canada" although it will probably be better remembered for Arthur Gropp's 'Toonarville Trolley'. More on that later.

The development of Key Harbour as an important port in the early 1900s began when a huge deposit of iron ore was discovered at Moose Mountain near Sudbury. The Moose Mountain Iron Mine opened. Since the mouth of the Key River provided the closest deep water harbour, this area was chosen as the mine's processing and shipping centre. Long docks, a cement powerhouse, a smelter, conveyor belts, tunnels, numerous houses, a boarding house, and a store were built. Railway tracks for a seven-mile (11.2-km) spur line from Key Junction (on the main line to Sudbury) to Key Harbour were laid. Key

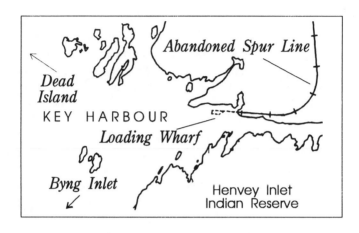

Refer to charts 2204, 2244

Harbour was in business.

Business, however, lasted only a decade. By 1916, it was apparent that Key Harbour was not deep enough to accommodate the newer, larger boats and so operations were relocated further south at Depot Harbour (page 109). Most of the ore facilities and docks were torn down. But Key Harbour received a reprieve from its impending ghost town status when the CNR chose it as a new coal port. Ships would deliver coal from American mines, and it would then be taken by rail to the northern Ontario mines, mills, and railroads.

Notwithstanding Key Harbour's spur line and its connections with the CNR, it was still a nightmare to get to

Key Harbour by land. Enter Arthur Gropp. Seeing that the railway tracks were used only occasionally for transporting coal, Arthur built a "jigger" by putting a Model-T engine on an old railway flatcar. He was soon chugging off to Key Junction and the main railroad whenever he jolly well pleased. His idea quickly caught on. He found himself driving hunters, Gauthier fishermen (see page 180) and their cargo, campers, tourists, and townspeople back and forth from the Junction to the Harbour. It wasn't the lounge car on a CNR passenger train, what with the occasional overhanging branch smacking an unwary passenger, the regular lurching of the jigger, and the intermittent delays of a moose or bear ambling along the tracks, but it did the job. Variations of the original trolley continued to be used for some forty years. In 1958, however, with the increase in automobile traffic, and the reduction of CNR passenger and freight service, the spur line was shut down and its tracks pulled up. Like the iron ore business, the coal business at Key Harbour was short-lived. Once again, the harbour proved too shallow for the newer, larger vessels. The demand for coal waned. Soon Key Harbour was without a sustainable industry.

All that is left of this port that once saw thousands of tons of coal flow through its gates are ruined wharves on the north shore. Dock pilings and the shell of the powerhouse can be seen from the water. Behind the store at the new dock, you can find the original boarding house, the abandoned rail bed (which you can follow if you are up to a hike), and rusting fragments of the railway era. Today the community is comprised mostly of summer cottagers.

Dead Island

The thrill-seeking crowd attending the 1893 World's Columbia Exposition in Chicago flocked to the year's big attraction: the opportunity to come face to face with an authentic North American Indian. 'See their mummified remains! Touch genuine sacred burial artifacts!!' Although a crowd pleaser, it was grave robbing, one of the most shameful acts committed on the Bay or anywhere. Dead Island's name derives from its use as an Indian burial ground. Ojibwa from the mainland brought their dead, wrapped them in blankets, furs, or sheets of birch bark with some of their belongings, and either placed them high in the trees or buried them deep under piles of large stones for protection against wild animals.

This may have kept the animals away, but it did nothing to deter a group of "entertainment" businessmen from Chicago, who were on a trip to discover new "attractions" for their exposition. When they heard an Indian burial ground existed on Dead Island, they landed on the island and stripped many of the grave sites of their occupants and personal belongings. And then it was back to Chicago to open the Exposition with their exciting and authentic new find. To be fair, many of the Victorians were genuinely interested in preserving "our vanishing history," but unfortunately for us, they wrought a substantial amount of archeological havoc in their day. No one knows what happened to the Dead Island remains after the exposition closed. Speculation has it that they were dumped into Lake Michigan.

An exhibit at the World's Columbia Exposition

The American archaeologist Emerson F. Greenman conducted several digs in the Killarney area in the 1930s, where he uncovered a number of Plano sites. The Plano were the first inhabitants of Georgian Bay dating back 10,000 years. Greenman also found what he believed was an old Algonkin burial ground on Little Birch Island, close to the La Cloche Islands (so named because a rock if struck will ring out like bell.) At the site he uncovered brass pails, iron knives, and blue beads hand painted with moons and stars. One item helped date the graves: a silver gorget engraved with a crown bearing the initials R.C.. Greenman traced R.C. to Robert Cruikshanks, a silversmith who had emigrated from London to Boston in 1768. Cruikshanks made silver items for trade with the natives in 1779. The artifacts on Little Birch were like many of those found on Ste. Marie II.

Bustard Islands

His energetic walk, his storytelling, and the twinkle in his eye gave us a few hints of the character of the men who once called these islands home for seven months of the year. Earlier in the day, we had picked him up at his cottage for our grand tour of the Bustards. A long-time Bustard resident and retired fisherman, Brian Drever took us back to a time when fishing shanties and skiffs and tugs dominated this rocky scene.

He showed us old shacks, an old ice crusher, dock cribbing, and the spot where there used to be a shanty before it was razed by the Ministry of Natural Resources; traces of the thriving fishing community which once boasted of bringing in over 6,000 pounds of fish in only a few days.

The Bustards were named after the slow-moving game bird of northwestern Europe known to gather in large flocks on isolated islands, remote from human contact. Unlike their namesake, the Bustard Islands saw plenty of humans, especially from 1880 to 1930. The 559 rocks and islands making up the Bustards were a busy spot for fishing whitefish, trout, and herring. Numerous skiffs zipped in and out of the cozy harbour - a harbour that would be the hub of commercial fishing for years. In 1875, the Dominion Fish Company established itself, using Ridout island, at the mouth of the Bustards' "Gun Barrel" entrance, as its main camp. The icehouse and supply dock were located here. Fishing families like the Pillgrems and Lowes built shanties and pack houses on islands from Green Island to Meaford Island.

In 1875 Edward B. Borron and his family came to man the small lighthouse erected west of the main group of Bustard Rocks. He tended the Bustard light for ten years and then his son took over for thirty-three. He was followed in 1919 by David Mountnay and in 1929 by Tommy Flynn. From 1875 to 1951, the lights were of the oilwick lamp type that had to be refilled daily. The central light was omnidirectional using a glass lens. William Campbell's book, *The French and Pickerel Rivers, Their History and Their People,* relates the story of Thomas Flynn, the last keeper before automation. While visiting a zoo Tom overheard a little girl ask her mother why the lion seemed agitated in its cage. "I'll tell you why," piped up Tom, "I keep the lights at the Bustard Rocks and I know what its like to pace up and down in a cage." One visit to the lighthouse will confirm Mr. Flynn's occupational plight. To make life on the rocks a little more pleasant, the Flynns transported 83 bushels of soil by boat in order to plant tomatoes, lettuce, carrots and other vegetables. He later brought chickens to his island and sold fresh eggs to visitors. Tom Flynn was a local legend for his humour, stories and expressions like "wouldn't that make you jump and grab your eyelashes;" and "couldn't drive a squirrel through with a black snake whip." When the sun

Vanished fishing station at Ridout Island, the Bustards

beats down on the ivory-coloured lighthouse, capped by its crimson roof, imagine the Flynn's small home once nestled alongside.

By the early 1930s, fishermen might have preferred sea monsters to the voracious sea lamprey that were sucking the life out of their fish stocks. Other forces contributed to the decline, but the result was that people pulled out and headed south, leaving only two commercial fishermen on the islands. By the mid-1950s they too left. Many of the fishing families, like the Pillgrems and the Drevers, continue to keep cottages here during the summer. More recently, the lure of sport fishing has brought people back to the Bustards, and each summer

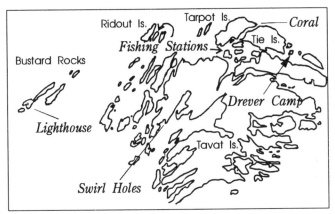

Refer to chart 2224

the area is host to numberless fishermen hoping to catch the "big one."

For those who don't fancy sitting in a boat and staring at the water for hours, there are fragments of history to be found on the Bustards' shores. A few of the remaining original fishing shanties have been made into summer cottages, and one is now a boat house. There is also an ice crusher, numerous cribs in the water and hooks on the rocks. Beneath the water's surface in the channel between Tarpot and Tie islands you can find the wreck of the sailboat *Coral*. It is an ideal wreck for families to explore together.

For an interesting diversion go to Tanvant Island and look at the pot-holes (locally called swirl-holes) in the bedrock. These perfectly round holes were carved out as the glaciers melted and formed fast-flowing streams. The streams would carry hard rocks, and deposit them in depressions in the granite. As the water continued to flow, the rock would swirl around and grind away at the granite, leaving what you see today. The smooth green hard rock is usually still at the bottom of the hole. (See chapter 4 for another theory on the creation of pot-holes)

French River

Long before the lumbermen laid claim to the river, the French was part of Canada's busiest fur trade highway. Around 1784, the North West Company made this river part of their fur trade canoe route between Montreal and Fort Chipewyan on Lake Athabasca. For thousands of years before that, it was a primary artery for many native groups. Its popularity was by no means based on its ease of navigation. This 78-mile (125-km) river is dotted with islands and shoals and is a series of rapids and falls. The magnetic pull of the river, especially at spots like Recollet Falls, Five Finger Rapids, Little and Big Pine Rapids, and the Dalles Rapids in Macdougal Bay has not lost its force.

French River Village Ghost Town

It was said French River Village could be sighted by following the heavy smoke from the 50-foot (15-m) stacks of its two mills. Today, however, it is hard to believe that a town whose population fluctuated from 200 to 1,400 — with its rows of two-story houses, two churches and schools, three hotels, barber shop and jail, all precariously

French River Village Hotel

perched on this rocky landscape — ever existed. As we plodded through the thick underbrush slipping and sliding on the wet rock, slapping away mosquitoes and keeping an eye out for poison ivy and rattlesnakes, it was clear that this would be the last place on Georgian Bay that we would choose to settle a town.

Apparently, we are made from different stock than Sam Wabb. In the early 1880s he settled here and opened a small trading post to service the modest lumber camps of the Walkerton Logging Company, established in the early 1870s. Not only was Mr. Wabb of hardy constitution but he was also of sound business mind. Observing that the existing bunkhouses were less than inviting after a hard day's labour in the woods, Wabb set about building eight shacks which he promptly rented out. They became known as Wabb Town and he became the area's first landlord. Inadvertently he helped lay out the early plans for the village of Coponaning, which would later evolve into the lively community of French River.

In the same year that Wabb collected his first rent payments, another tenacious soul arrived on the shores of French River. His name was Herman H. Cook, and he had heard that the Walkerton Company was faltering. Something he found hard to believe considering the rich supply of pine along these shores. Cook bought the Walkerton mill and its timber license and formed the

French River Village from the south

Ontario Lumber Company. From this mill came one of the largest lumber operations the Bay would ever see.

What was unique about the entrepreneurs of this era was the need not only to create a viable business, but also the entire infrastructure to go with it. In the case of Cook, first he built two mills and then he surveyed the site of the future town (See Depot Harbour). By 1900, rows of buildings stretched along the rocky cliffs behind the mills; houses were built anywhere and everywhere to accommodate French River's expanding population. Crammed onto inhospitable jagged rocks, crags, and ledges, the houses had long staircases leading down to 'the road' — a somewhat flatter "channel" cutting through the rock and covered with sawdust. Massive piles of lumber crowded the docks and yards. Work was steady, there was food on the table, life was good.

The proprietors of the three hotels were always guaranteed profitable Saturday nights with the lumbermen in need of spirits. They also began to cater to the tourist by offering attractive hunting and fishing trips and evenings topped off with fine brandy, wine and cigars... or perhaps a gentlemanly game of billiards. Each day the steamer *Norbelle* left Collingwood packed with curious sightseers, hunters, and fishermen on their way to enjoy French River.

A decade later, production at the mill declined. French River fishermen, most of them working for Gauthier (see Gauthier Fisheries), grumbled about sawdust in the Bay which was ruining fish spawning beds. Fishermen all over the Bay were complaining. By 1910, a pollution control law was passed curtailing this practice

French River Village, built on the rocks

and other environmentally-unfriendly activities. Mills began to close. The two industries, fishing and lumbering, which kept this part of the Bay humming for so long were about to disappear. To make matters worse, the timber supply was dwindling. Railways were rapidly replacing shipping as the transport of choice. But there were no plans to extend the new railway line to French River. The Ontario Lumber Company went into receivership, and in 1912, the Pine Lake Lumber Company bought the mills and moved them to a better location on Pickerel River. As quickly as the town had appeared, it disappeared, just packed up and left.

A determined few stayed. The Wabb store operated until 1922, the post office until 1923, and a light keeper

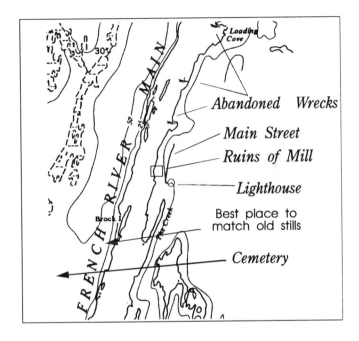

Refer to chart 2204, sheet 2

stayed with his light at the mouth of the river. They served the handful of fishermen, trappers and loggers set on making it here on their own. The story about the lighthouse keeper Bob Young illustrates the strength of character necessary to live in a place as remote as the deserted French River. In the early 1930s, Bob and his wife were the only ones left. They operated the lighthouse and kept a watchful eye on the ghost town. During a particularly bad winter, Mrs. Young died. Bob was unable to bury her in the frozen ground and kept her coffin outside until people were able to come in the spring to help take her away for a proper burial.

Two years after the mill was moved, the York Wrecking Company demolished most of the village. It was a sound business decision as the empty buildings were an insurance liability. From an historical perspective, it was a loss to the Bay. Those buildings not dismantled were left to rot. Trees and shrubs took root in the sawdust and reclaimed their land.

The foundation of the old mill with the chimney stack is still standing, slightly obscured from view by trees and bushes. The crumbling stone foundations of the warehouse, jail and powerhouse still exist, and all kinds of debris are scattered along the shore and through the bush — boilers, buckets, bricks, and metal bits. Rusty hooks used to tie up incoming vessels can be found pounded into the shoreline rocks, while boilers, a few abandoned boats and cribbing from the old dock lie under the water. There is a small graveyard across the river (see map). The lighthouse is still standing and in operation.

To fully enjoy this site, and to compare "what is" with "what was," it is a good idea to take along a few old photographs or maps (William Campbell's *The French And Pickeral Rivers, Their History and Their People* is a good source for photos.) Go ashore across the river from the lighthouse and line up the lighthouse and mill with help of the photograph, keeping in mind that water levels have varied up to six feet (1.8m) over the years. The shoreline is fairly easy to explore. The main road through the village

French River

might be a little more difficult, as it is quite overgrown. The dip in the land up from the water is the former main road, where rows of houses once stood. Be prepared for mosquitoes and blackflies, especially in the dense bush, as well as poison ivy. If it's raining, the rocky terrain can become quite slippery. And, of course, there is always the rattler warning... something we had not taken seriously. Our guard down, we blithely strolled into a basking Massasauga at French River. Thank goodness the dislike was mutual, and he slithered off.

Bad River Channel

For over seventy years, beginning in 1896, the archipelago in this winding river was not only home to abundant blueberries, seagulls, snakes, juniper, and the occasional hardy tree, but to the men who worked for Gauthier Fishery. At the time, Charles Gauthier ran the largest private fishing operation on the Bay. The first camp was built in 1896 on an island in the west channel of Bad River. In 1916, Gauthier leased an island on the eastern side of Bad River channel where it opens into Georgian Bay, north northwest of the Bustard Islands. His fishery grew into a sizable operation that included sixteen employees, who kept a

Bad River fishing camp, 1909

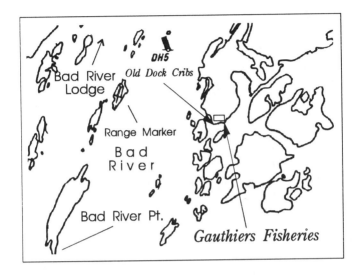

Refer to charts 2204, 2244

sixty foot tug, two scows, a tow boat and four fishing boats busy. Their nets were imported from Scotland and sized in Toronto. When fishing fell off in the 1950s and 1960s, Charles's son Faulconer left the industry and the sprawling fishery was dismantled. Today at Bad River, you'll find only a handful of sport fishermen, but the scenery is still there. And its worth the trip.

Hallelujah Rock
Pioneer Farm

William Campbell tells of a mystery located on "Hallelujah" Rock, a smooth rock island in Chaughis Bay. In 1974, two Salvation Army officers discovered a curious inscription carved into the rock, 'Salvation Army 1898.' No one knows its origin, although Campbell and some local residents speculate that the Salvation Army held services during the summer on this island for either the loggers or surrounding native families.

Through the bush north of the rock can be found the remains of a farm built in the late 1800s. John Gahgahke and his wife started the farm on which they raised horses, chickens, pigs, and cattle. They grew vegetables and hunted deer, moose and partridge - their table was not lacking. He and his wife died in the 1920s and are buried on the farm. There is little left but the remains of the house and barn, as well as old farm tools scattered in the overgrown meadows.

NOTE: *To locate these two sites be ready for rough weather. The stretch of water from Bad River to Beaverstone Bay is often turbulent for weeks at a time and the shoals are legendary. Traveling in a large boat or sailboat is not recommended and be prepared with accurate charts.*

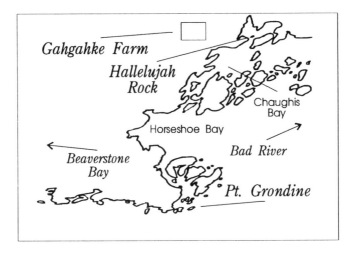

Refer to charts 2204, 2244

Point Grondine

North of Bad River a piece of land juts out into the open Bay. This is Point Grondine, so named by local natives because of the low, roaring sound made by the churning waves (*grondeur* means rumbling.) This point was a difficult hurdle for the voyageurs and their cumbersome canoes to overcome. They often waited weeks for a day calm enough to round the point and to reach the shelter of Beaverstone Bay.

At the northeast corner of Beaverstone Bay can be seen a two-story farmhouse made of hand hewn logs that was built in the 1920s by the Ukrainian immigrant and former lumberman, Steven Paterek. He and his wife Maria toiled in isolation for years to create a sizable farm, where they and their three children, Frank, Helen and Steven, could live off the fruits of their labour. Maria's love for the homestead never faltered - through her eighties she could still be seen tending the garden. Today the old house is a poignant symbol of our pioneers' strength and determination.

Collins Inlet Ghost Town
Early Logging Life

The job description read: minimal pay; long hours; all

Lumber Shanty

weather; all seasons; back-breaking labour; life threaten-ing; cramped and dirty living conditions; and no women. Yet they still came - hundreds of lumber men streamed into Georgian Bay's virgin forests. Not listed were: black-leg, or landlubber's scurvy - a horrible affliction caused by eating only salted pork sandwiches smothered in corn syrup for breakfast, lunch, and dinner; swarms of black flies, deer flies, and horseflies; and mosquitoes "as big as horses" (and "by Jobe they'll eat yeah alive.") Day in and day out they felled the forest; driving the logs down the rivers during the spring melt. To be a lumber man, strength and endurance were the only requirements. The job attracted many new immigrants and consequently lumber camps became mini United Nations. Some camps developed strange rituals such as enforcing complete silence for all the men during mealtimes. Their sleeping quarters were log cabins, where they squeezed into crude-ly constructed wooden bunks. After a sweaty day's work, only their boots were removed before sleeping. They stretched their wool-socked feet towards the blazing cen-tral fire which choked the room with smoke.

Personal hygiene was not a priority - after all, the female persuasion was not allowed "a tornado's-tail length" near a camp. This rule led to a few practical jokes. In John Macfie's excellent *Parry Sound Logging Days,* he writes about a cook who bought himself a pair of fancy women's high-heeled shoes. When everyone was asleep, he walked outside, leaving crisp impressions in the fresh snow. The next morning the men were "whinner'n and whistle'n," desperately looking for this phantom woman, and the red faced foreman was holler'n, "there was a

Collins Inlet mill

women in the place and no woman has no damned business be'n here!"

The lumber industry sank its hooks and axes into the lower regions of the Bay in the early 1870s. Log booms as wide as 25 acres (40ha) made traveling by water at night life threatening. Starvation Bay, on the eastern shore, became legendary after a poor fellow was stranded there in his boat for a week, thanks to a massive log boom blocking the entrance to Georgian Bay. Along with all the cut wood came the mill towns. When times were good, towns rose almost over night. When times were tough, ghost towns appeared just as quickly. And such is the story of Collins Inlet, one of the most northern ghost towns along the Bay.

In 1886, entrepreneur John Bertram came to the Inlet. He took over a small mill that prepared timber coming down from La Cloche for shipment to the south. He named his enterprise the Collins Inlet Lumber Company, and built a small town adjacent to the mill. A boarding house, many private homes, a company store, and a school soon encircled the 100-foot sawdust burner. At one time the town of Collins Inlet was home to more than 200 people.

When Bertram died in 1904 the mill and town continued to prosper. It was fortunate he was not alive in 1918. It would have been painful for him to watch the mill be destroyed by fire, and then picked over by salvagers for metal to feed the First World War furnaces. The property was sold; the lumber operation moved to Midland, and the town site left to rot. The schooners sank into the Inlet, and the shores grew silent.

The past mixes with the present at Collins Inlet. A few resilient buildings from the town still stand and have become part of a hunting and fishing camp called the Mahzenazing River Lodge. Guests at the lodge and others who get permission can explore the ruins of the mill, burner, and docks. The Lodge has converted the former company boarding house into a guest house.

Access to the town site, and anywhere along Collins Inlet, is by boat only. Canoeing is recommended as the preferred pace, as it allows time to spot a hawk or a heron, to drink it all in. Leaving Killarney, follow the shoreline to the rock-walled protection of the Philip Edward Channel leading into Mill Lake. Charts are necessary to locate the

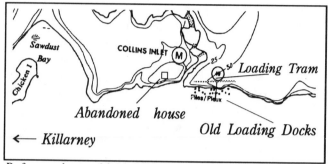

Refer to charts 2244, 2204

townsite from the water and to guide you past the inlet's copious shoals. Passing Sawdust Bay, you round a point, revealing an old red two-story wooden house with a green roof on the left as you travel east. Past that house there is a second one tucked in the bush on a hill. Even further east from the present lodge dock lie the remains of the town dock where schooners and steamers once moored and where townspeople awaited the twice-weekly delivery of news and mail.

The road leading up from the dock passes the ruins of the mill and burner. Further along the road is the clearing where Mr. Bertram's town once stood, and where the original boarding house, now the lodge stands. If you want to stay longer than a day there are designated camp-sites spread throughout the area. The inlet is Crown land, so sites cannot be reserved: it is first-come, first-served.

Killarney
Killarney Provincial Park

Centuries ago, before the Ontario government recognized the value of this beautiful and pristine wilderness and sought to preserve it, the Ojibwa honoured this land by calling it "Heaven's Gate," a land of great spirits, guarded by a magical raven. It was a place to receive visions and advice from the gods, a place for contemplation. Today, many of us use it for similar purposes, to get away from city life, to gain perspective. There is something undeniably magical in these white quartzite mountains, their surrounding granite shoreline and deep green waters.

Shebahonaning, before it became Killarney

The first people to be attracted to these shores were the semi-nomadic Plano, who set up camp in the Killarney area some 10,000 years ago. They made primitive tools and hunting weapons from the strong splinters of white quartzite they chipped off the La Cloche mountains. Then came the Woodland Indians, the Hopewell, the Peninsula Woodland Indians, the Laronde, and the Copper Indians. Sometime between 1640 to 1760 A.D., the Algonkian-speaking peoples (also called the Chippewa, Ojibwa, and Ottawa) came into the area. Like their southern Huron neighbours, they were soon to meet their first white men, fur traders. By 1759, one of the main fur trading routes passed through the area. After fighting their way through the rough water of the open Bay, voyageurs looked forward to reaching Shebahonaning (Algonkin for "safe canoe channel" and Killarney's early name.)

Life at Shebahonaning was quite transient until the arrival, in June 1820, of businessman and fur trader Etienne Augustin de la Morandiere, who set up a tidy little trading post. He was the area's first farmer — growing potatoes, corn, and wheat — and cattle owner (he shipped the cattle over from Manitoulin Island). People began to settle around his trading post, and the community of Shebahonaning was born. In the early years, Shebahonaning was primarily a fishing community. Being so isolated, the men had to knit their own nets, often from cotton and linen unraveled from clothing.

The word Shebahonaning was still quite a mouthful for most residents. According to Kevin Callan in his book, *Killarney*, sometime in the mid-1840s, town merchant Robert Johnston suggested the name be changed to

Killarney. Others believe Lady Dufferin, on her 1874 tour of Ontario with her husband, Lord Dufferin, suggested the name be changed to Killarney because it reminded her of Killarney, Ireland. A stamp dated 1848 bearing the Killarney name tends to support Mr. Johnston's story.

Like the surrounding area, Killarney prospered from the logging and fishing industries, adding a dash of silica mining near Willisville and on Badgeley Island for good measure. Mirroring the fate of other regions, fishing was curtailed by logging pollution, over fishing, and the sea lamprey's appetite. By 1960, commercial fishing in Killarney had collapsed. Today, there are only a few full-time fishermen casting nets into these waters.

Even though commercial fishing suffered, Killarney's reputation as "a good fishing hole" still reached the ears of wealthy American sportsmen, who were lured northward in search of prime sport fishing and hunting. After years of boat access only, a road was built from Highway 69 to Killarney in 1962, heralding its next phase: tourism.

Killarney's ancient mountains have attracted some special people over the years. The first official tourist was Anna B. Jameson, author of *Winter Studies and Summer Rambles in Canada*. In 1833, she made a trip through Georgian Bay in two twenty-five foot canoes, fully decked out with parasol and eau de cologne. Her guides were seven strapping voyageurs who shattered the frontiersmen stereotype: "The seven Voyageurs sat behind Martin the Indian Steersman who wore loose trousers, a scarlet sash which was richly embroidered with beads.... On an island abounded with beautiful flowers, green mosses and scarlet lichen I found a tiny recess where I made my bath.

Anna B. Jameson visiting Killarney in 1830s

On return I found my breakfast laid on a piece of rock with my pillow and cloak, nicely arranged with a bouquet of flowers lying on it."

Other famous guests included: John Gutzon Borghum, the sculptor of Mt. Rushmore; and the Group of Seven, in particular Frank Carmichael, Arthur Lismer, A.J. Casson, and A.Y. Jackson. And then there were the infamous: In 1946, a Mr. Fruehauf built a luxury retreat for his clients, complete with airstrip. He would fly them in, take them hunting or fishing, fill them full of fresh country air and good cooking and then talk business. Some of this business turned out to be questionable. Investigations by the IRS over his dealings with Teamster Jimmy Hoffa led to his selling the resort in the 1960s. It is now the Killarney Mountain Lodge.

As the gateway to the North Channel and beyond, Killarney is now at ease with its tourism role. The Killarney Provincial Park is considered one of Ontario's best kept secrets, a 121,250 acre (48,500ha) wilderness park with hiking trails, campsites, and canoe routes, all offering tranquillity and solitude. There is still sport fishing in the Bay, although Park wardens discourage fishing in park lakes due to the impact of acid rain. The Killarney Museum, located in a log house one block from the dock, is worth a visit, especially if you are interested in the area's early fishing days.

This area has dive sites with geological interest as well as a few man-made sites. Although the man-made sites lack some of the imagination and mystery of sites in Fathom Five, for example, they are easy to dive on. They are located on the south side of Badgley Island, near the Indusmin Silica Mine. Follow the ledge down the silica wall 120 feet (36m) to a fascinating underwater landscape of rocks, ledges, and slopes. Other Killarney area dive sites include various shipwrecks and automobiles. To get information on locating them inquire at the Sportsman Inn.

India Wreck

One wreck worth visiting is the *India*, just north of Killarney and west of Mary Island. This 976-ton wooden propeller ship was built in 1899 and burned September 4,

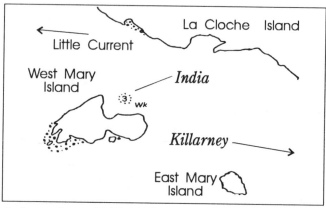

Refer to charts 2205, 2245

1929. Now it provides habitat for sunfish and perch. It is in 10 to 25 feet (3m to 7.5m) of water and is safe in all conditions. An easy find.

The Squaw Island Fishing Station
Sea Monsters

The promise of $5 a month was all it took to lure eager young men up to the remote fishing stations along the Bay's northern shores. An extra $50 guaranteed they would stay all season. And they came in droves. As predictable as geese flying south for the winter was the flock of fishermen and their families migrating north for the summer to the fishing colonies scattered on these islands.

Although there had always been local fishing on the Bay, it was not until 1875 that commercial fishermen took a serious interest. Word spread about the abundance of whitefish, trout, and chub just waiting to be caught. Who could resist such an opportunity? There was one rumour of a man who, from the proceeds of selling just one sturgeon, was able to buy a fine suit, a gallon of whisky, and a cow.

Bringing in the sturgeon

One of the biggest stations in this area was Squaw Island. In its heyday, its southern shores were dotted with shanties housing anywhere from 60 to 80 fishermen and their families from all over — Collingwood, Lion's Head, Meaford, and Killarney. Many of the Collingwood fishermen who gravitated to Squaw Island were recent emigrants from Scotland. By 1903, the island was the fishing hub of the northwest Bay. It boasted 50 skiffs, three tugs, a school and a summer mission.

Fishermen were pulling in 10 to 15 tons of fish a week, and selling it to the hungry markets of New York, Detroit, Philadelphia, and Cleveland. It was busy during the season but the Squaw Station boys still had time to challenge the fishermen from Club Island and Killarney to a sailboat race. Life was good, according to old-time fisherman, John Hillis. "Although you worked long hours setting and hauling and repairing nets; and salting, drying and freezing fish; with a good-sized community on the island, you were always guaranteed a party or two, not to mention a few practical jokes. Although the company store ended up taking a lot of your money for supplies, there was a little change left over for the winter." By 1916, as in other parts of the Bay, dwindling fish stocks reduced Squaw Island to fewer than 20 men.

By the mid-1930s, two other factors ensured the demise of the fishing industry: the introduction of the sea lamprey eel into Georgian Bay waters by foreign boats, and the large increase in smelt. Fishermen could not combat the lamprey's relentless appetite (or its rapid reproduction rate), as it sucked the blood out of large numbers of trout. Meanwhile trout were devouring the indigestible smelt which turned their insides green. Fishermen watched as their profits were literally eaten up before their eyes. By 1940, a few faithful tugs remained in the waters. By 1950, commercial fishing off this island had stopped completely.

Mackinaw regattas were popular among fishermen

Who knows if it was during the low periods - when fishermen had a bit of time on their hands - or during the peak years - when they were working so hard they were hallucinating - but it seems that throughout the Bay, fishermen have reported sighting sea-monsters. They were supposedly sighted at Vail's Point, at Manitoulin, the Limestones, and Gull Island. The descriptions varied from a creature about four feet long, with four feet, fins, and reddish cauliflower-shaped knobs on its sides - to a man with fins and a tail. Some turned out to be submerged logs, or exceptionally large sturgeon. One fisherman sent his catch away to Ottawa for identification. The Ministry of Natural Resources identified it as a mudpuppy. A young

An average Georgian Bay catch

girl on the Bustard Islands casually looked out the window
and announced she could see a shark. Her grandfather
ignored her until she insisted he look. He agreed there
was something strange, and a quick check revealed a very
dead four-foot shark lying on an island with an apple in its
mouth.

Lake Huron fishermen ,1909

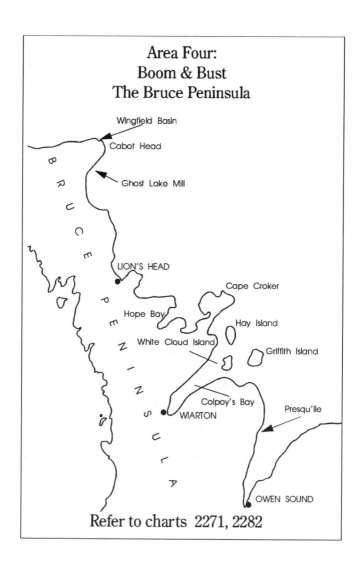

Area Four:
Boom & Bust
The Bruce Peninsula

Wingfield Basin

Cabot Head

Ghost Lake Mill

BRUCE

LION'S HEAD

Cape Croker

Hope Bay

Hay Island

White Cloud Island

Griffith Island

PENINSULA

Colpoy's Bay

Presqu'ile

WIARTON

OWEN SOUND

Refer to charts 2271, 2282

4

Boom and Bust : The Bruce Peninsula

As we traveled north along the Bruce Peninsula, we were confident our search for this area's ghosts would be effortless. For it seemed that along these jagged bluffs, time had been locked into its limestone faces, its history just waiting to be revealed. The Bruce changes for no one - not even the monumental forces of the Ice Age could crush her great spine. She shares her scars; the remains of her prehistoric forests both above and below the water; many natural and manmade monuments; and early "boom towns" that continue to prosper even today.

We quickly discovered that the Bruce is perhaps the Bay's most mysterious shore, home to unfound wrecks and lost souls, unsolved murders and hidden identities, wily gangs of counterfeiters and bootleggers. Some of the story began at our first stop, Owen Sound.

Owen Sound

On surveyor Gother Mann's 1788 map, Owen Sound appeared as Thunder Bay. It is said that during storms, thunder would echo up and down both sides of the bay. Local surveyor Charles Rankin renamed the bay Sydenham in 1840, after Lord Sydenham, Governor-in-Chief of Canada at the time. It was subsequently renamed Owen Sound, not after Captain William Fitzwilliam Owen as everyone assumes, but after his brother, Admiral Sir Edward William Campbell Rich Owen. Its nickname would later become Corkscrew City, and you can bet that it earned it.

In the earliest days, whiskey arrived in one of two ways: it was delivered by horse, or bootleggers snuck it in by boat and cached it along the shore. By the time it was a twelve-shanty hamlet, it already boasted two taverns. By 1844, it was described as 'a rough town of log shanties where drunks and hogs stumbled along the street.'

One night in 1844, when tempers were quick and judgment was cloudy, one George Ferguson and William Douglas began to argue about politics, religion, women and who bought the last drink. The origin of the argument has never been determined but its result has been extensively documented – the two men agreed to meet the following day and settle their differences.

Two rather pale young men showed up at the designated spot at the agreed upon time, each with a friend and a pistol. Fifty paces were measured out, the pistols were examined, and the men took their positions. When the smoke cleared two stunned gentlemen stared incredu-

Owen Sound, 1915

lously at each other as they checked for wounds. Relieved to discover that neither had been shot, they smiled and embraced, and took off to the nearest tavern to cement their new found friendship with a little brandy.

In 1857, Owen Sound boasted a population of 2,000 and was incorporated as a town. When the Toronto-Grey and Bruce Railway arrived in 1873, Owen Sound was on its way to becoming one of the largest and most important transshipping centres on the Bay. Around this time the name Corkscrew City began to be heard. If you weren't buying liquor in the taverns, you were making "Raisin Jack" in your bathtub. One moonshiner ran a still in the cliffs of the Peninsula for years. He made rum and whiskey out of molasses, a spring supplied the water and an old hollow cedar stump served as a chimney. If anyone came snooping around his site, the moonshiner would send his son out to sit nonchalantly on the stump.

In Andrew Armitage's *Owen Sound: The Day the Governor General Came to Town*, he notes that charges of "irregularities" were being added to Owen Sound's growing reputation as the "fightenest, drunkenest, whoringest town in Ontario." Fake bills, plug nickels, and false notes of unknown origin appeared. There was even, at one time, an unlikely poisoner on the loose. A widow who married her dead husband's hired hand five days after the burial was accused of poisoning. Enough eyebrows were raised to exhume her husband's body and do a post-mortem examination. The symptoms of strychnine poisoning were detected, but no actual traces of the poison were found. One wonders if her second husband slept very well at night.

Despite all the carryings-on, Owen Sound also managed to build a reputable name as a shipbuilding centre. The *Ann Mackenzie*, one of the first commercial ships built on the Bay, was launched in Owen Sound in 1846. She was followed by the *Elizabeth Broder,* the *Belle McPhee,* the *Ploughboy* (p. 290), the *Frances Smith* and countless others. The *Caribou, Manitou, Manitoulin, Manasoo*, the *Hibou*, and the *Normac* would also become familiar names in this port. In 1884, the CPR bought out the Toronto-Grey and Bruce Railway and chose Owen Sound as the railway base for its new steamship line. The CPR years were prosperous ones. Cargo vessels carried everything from lumber to grain to escaped slaves from Chicago during the early 1850s. Passenger steamers were popular, especially those on the "Turkey Trail," so named because of the haphazard route they took, dodging reefs, shoals and islands, to service ports from Owen Sound to Lake Superior via the upper Bay and North Channel. These small steamers called in at fishing stations along the Bay, bringing supplies and returning with fish for the southern markets.

Competition was fierce between the two ports of Collingwood and Owen Sound, in particular between Collingwood's Black Pete Campbell (p. 159) and Owen Sound's Neil Campbell. Each pushed the other to go faster, to take greater risks, until finally passengers began to complain. An editorial in the August 1, 1889 *Owen Sound Advertiser* declared, "The officers and crews of these boats may possibly enjoy this kind of work, but we are pretty sure those who travel with them do not. People go out on these excursions to enjoy themselves, not to be terrorized and run the risk of losing their lives." The end to this rivalry came when the *Carmona* and the *Baltic,* both full of passengers, engaged in a race so close that the two ships actually bumped together numerous times.

With the development of the Owen Sound Transportation Company, the town enjoyed its reputation as an important transshipping centre for over thirty years, until trucks and automobiles became the transport of choice. One by one, steamers left the Bay for good, some were scrapped, some foundered, some like the *Caribou* and the *Normac* were turned into restaurants. The ship-building yards closed. Today only the familiar *Chi-Cheemaun* is around to remind us of this vibrant era.

The County of Grey-Owen Sound Museum has a comprehensive display of life in Owen Sound between 1815 and 1920. The Marine and Rail Museum captures the history of these two powerful industries, while the Billy Bishop Heritage Home and Museum, and the Tom Thompson Memorial Art Gallery commemorate outstanding Owen Sound residents. Other points of interest for hikers or photographers are the scenic recreational park lands found in the Inglis Falls Conservation Area and the Indian Falls Conservation Area, both part of the Bruce Trail.

Hibou Conservation Area

Now a welcome sight for picnickers, the Hibou Conservation Area's two sandy beaches were once a haven for survivors of a devastating shipping tragedy. The conservation area, overlooking Paynter's Bay on Owen Sound Bay, was named after the *Hibou*, a freighter that sank mysteriously off these shores on November 21, 1936. Loaded with hay, flour, and other supplies for the Manitoulin Island communities, the *Hibou* left Owen Sound on schedule and in clear weather.

Within twenty minutes, she was rapidly taking in water. Seven people were trapped on board. Those who managed to escape swam to the south of Squaw Point. From the safety of the Gibbons' home, they watched the *Hibou* sink into 80 feet (24m) of water. Were there other survivors? The next morning, heavy waves washed the bodies ashore, including that of the *Hibou's* Captain,

The Hibou, foundered 1936

Norman McKay, president of the Owen Sound Transportation Company, reputedly one of the best marine men on the Great Lakes. (The *Hibou* was raised in 1942, rebuilt, and used as a fruit boat in Florida.)

Presqu'ile

John Mackenzie was a true entrepreneur for whom the word "dollar" was found between "supply" and "demand" in the dictionary. In 1873 the Bay was crowded with steamers all needing cordwood for fuel. Mackenzie chose Presqu'ile (almost an island) as a perfect site to open his late nineteenth-century "gas station". It was nine miles (14.4km) north of Owen Sound and covered with old growth forest. Mackenzie built a 400-foot (121m) wharf, a lighthouse, a warehouse, and hired men to haul cordwood from the woods. In his first year of operation, over 136 ships leaving Owen Sound stopped here to refuel. Presqu'ile soon boasted a population of nearly four hundred people - four hundred very sober people, as Presqu'ile was declared a temperance zone. Land lots were sold on the condition that no liquor was to be used on the premises or in the village. Apparently Mackenzie had had enough of the shenanigans of his "spirited" neighbour (see Owen Sound.)

Presqu'ile's short history did include its requisite fifteen minutes of fame when, in 1874, Lord and Lady Dufferin included the town on their Georgian Bay tour itinerary. Like many of the Bay's boom towns, progress built Presqu'ile and then destroyed it. As steamers switched from wood to coal for their fuel Mackenzie turned to tourism. He created an amusement park with an "Ariel Railway," a primitive roller coaster devised from a small car that ran back and forth on a 200-foot cable suspended between two platforms. "Five cents for the thrill of your life!" was the pitch, but the attractions slowly wore off. All that is left of Mackenzie's dreams is the lightkeeper's house which was renovated in the 1950s by Cecil Corfe. The property and cottage now belong to the Rotary Club.

Presqu'ile Lighthouse

Nahneebahweequay

En route to England, the ship cuts through the cold grey Atlantic Ocean. Passengers can't help but notice the small, dark-haired woman of aboriginal descent in the dining room. Comments pass discreetly amongst the passengers, "She seems to be traveling alone..." "she looks to be in a "family way..." "Why would she be going to England, unattended?" No one could guess that this Georgian Bay woman was going to bring international attention to Canadian native land claims, and had arranged a meeting with the Queen.

Although small in stature, Nahneebahweequay

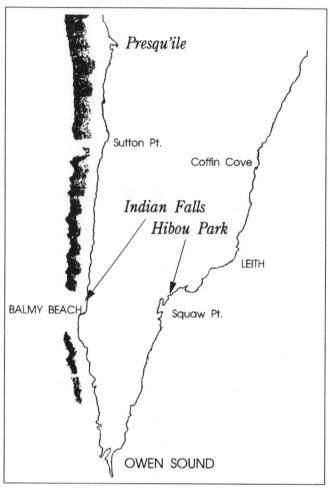

Refer to charts 2271, 2282

Catharine Sutton

(Upright Woman) or Catharine Sutton (her married name) was a determined woman. Born to Chief Senegal, Nahnee had been adopted by her uncle, Reverend Peter Jones, and had converted to Methodism in 1825. She journeyed to England to pursue an education and, upon her return to Canada, worked as a missionary. In 1839, she married lay minister William Sutton. They worked together as missionaries with the Newash Band around Port Credit. Around 1844, the Port Credit natives presented them with a 600 acre (240ha) parcel of land (now known as Sarawack Township) in appreciation of their sacrifice and service. Here the Suttons built a house and a barn with surrounding cherry and apple orchards.

It was 1851, and development pressures brought increasing demands for land to build roads and settlements. Original Indian "deeds" to the area were being ignored by European immigrants and many natives were to lose their land, the Suttons' property included. The natives arranged council meetings to try to negotiate with their new "neighbours," but to no avail. In 1857, the Indian lands were put up on the auction block. The Ojibwa scraped together money in order to attend the auction to buy back what was theirs but they were ignored. Worse was yet to come. A treaty forced the removal of all the Newash from the area to a reserve at Cape Croker. If something were not done the situation might take a violent turn. Catherine was despairing, but she believed that somewhere there must be justice and honour.

She had been an active participant in the campaign for Indian rights, but her most powerful endeavour was to arrange a meeting with the Queen of England. Catherine's visit in 1860 was well-documented by the press. Wherever she went she made a favourable impression. One account recalled the time she walked into the bar car of a train, full of the usual upper-class passengers of the time, and "charmed the room" with her graciousness and soft-spoken manner.

Catharine's visit with Queen Victoria lasted twenty minutes. She presented the Queen with gifts and described the plight and injustices suffered by her people. The Queen appeared sympathetic, stating, "I am happy to promise you my aid and protection." Catharine was given a promise that the Duke of Newcastle and the Prince of Wales would look into the situation on their next visit to Canada. Catharine was grateful. When her son was born she named him Albert after the Prince. She remained in England for a year then returned to Canada eagerly waiting for the royal visit.

The Duke eventually came to Georgian Bay but after a brief meeting with government and Indian leaders he declared the matter a provincial responsibility and washed his "Royal hands of the matter." The Suttons were awarded sixty dollars and approximately 200 (80ha) of their 600 acres (240ha) were returned to them, because the Queen was fond of this "woman of yellow colour." This was an empty gesture for Catharine as the others received nothing. Broken by false promises from a deceitful government, she succumbed to a respiratory illness four years later in 1865. Presqu'ile is the humble burial place of this famous Indian woman. Her grave at Wadineedinon is tended by members of the County Grey Historical Society in loving memory of her strong will and search for justice.

Colpoy's Bay
Prehistoric Forest

Natives called this bay Wahshushweequaid, meaning "bay of muskrats." Even though the muskrats are now gone, the town of Wiarton is home to the famed groundhog, Willie, who predicts winter's final curtain call. Along with Wiarton Willie, many other curiosities and treasures can be found in Colpoy's Bay and beyond: old mansions, unsolved murders, suicides... and ghosts - ghost ships, ghost lakes... ghosts galore.

Colpoy's Bay is dominated by the strong form of the Bruce Peninsula which splits the blue waters of Georgian Bay from the clear blue sky. Biologists prize this crumbling limestone embankment. Clinging to the thin soil is some of the last virgin forest left in Ontario - but don't look for giant trees - what grows here is a miniature primeval tree. At 400 years of age, this gnarled cedar looks like Mother Nature's own bonsai tree. In a less likely place stands another ancient forest - this one 8,000 years old. In the silent waters at the mouth of Colpoy's Bay, spongy stumps (some still with bark,) look like miniature volcanoes about two feet (1.2m) in height, and cover an area the size of a football field. Scientists believe this submerged forest grew when the retreating glaciers blocked the flow of water into the Great Lakes. At this time, the water would have been 100 feet (30m) below the level seen today. When the basin refilled, the forest was trapped in time.

The Jane Miller Mystery

Some say that the Bay is possessive of her spoils. She does have many captives in her vast crypt - her most precious being, perhaps, the *Asia* and the *Jane Miller*. Occasionally an eerie grave marker for the *Jane Miller's* twenty-eight lost lives reappears, making her the only ghost ship on the Bay.

On the evening of November 25, 1881, the heavily-laden steamer, the *Jane Miller*, was on her way from

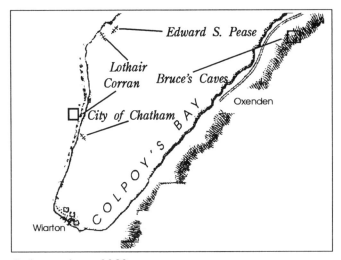

Refer to chart 2282

Owen Sound to Wiarton when she stopped at Big Bay to load on wood for fuel. As she left Big Bay, a blinding snow-storm swept in. Not one to be intimidated by a "little snow," the captain stubbornly pushed on.

At one point she was spotted struggling through the storm by Rod Cameron from his family home on Cameron's Point. He strained to keep sight of her, but she disappeared, engulfed by the white sheets of snow. That was the last seen of her. Somewhere in the ten miles (16km) between docks, she simply rolled over, taking her cargo and crew down perhaps 220 feet (66m) to rest at the bottom of Colpoy's Bay.

When the storm had passed, searchers following

Jane Miller, Georgian Bay's only ghost ship.

Cameron's directions combed the area where she was last sighted, not quite knowing what to expect. One group discovered the dreaded evidence on White Cloud Island: oars with her name on them, a broken flagstaff, her fire-bucket rack, and five cloth caps. McGregor and a group of friends joined the search in a rowboat. They found a clue - large oily black, bubbles rising up from the depths. The search crews began the final process of dragging the lake bottom. It should only have taken a few hours to find her resting place. They dragged. They dragged again. And again. And never found the wreck.

Twenty-five years later, in 1907, a group of hunters were sitting around a campfire on White Cloud Island

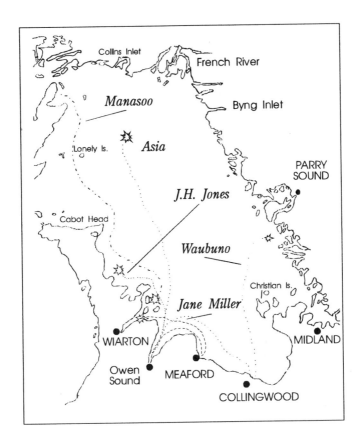

Mysterious Disappearances on Georgian Bay

when they heard eerie, distant and pained cries for help. The cries seemed to roll off the black night waves and then be swallowed by them. They sat around the fire, stunned, waiting for morning light so they could leave. On the Bay, they sailed through a peculiar sight - an oily patch of water that seemed to be bubbling up from the darkest depths of the Bay. The spot lined up perfectly with Rod Cameron's house.

Where is the *Jane Miller?* No one knows for sure. Perhaps she is where they believe her to be - only trapped inside a deep underwater chasm where the Bruce Peninsula meets the bottom of the Georgian Bay basin. The unsolved mystery of the *Jane Miller* is only one of the many connected with Colpoy's Bay. Both Griffith Island and White Cloud Island have their secrets, and their skeletons as well.

Griffith And White Cloud Islands

When three skeletons, two with crushed skulls, were unearthed from shallow graves on Griffith Island at the turn of the century, people were sure that a thirty-year murder mystery had finally been solved. It involved four men - Charles Fothergill, a Wiarton landowner; John Robinson, an American living in Owen Sound; George Brown, Owen Sound's postmaster (and his dog); and Charles Kennedy, an invalid sailor. In September 1869, Fothergill left Wiarton to do some banking and shopping in Owen Sound. After withdrawing $2,000 and loading his boat with farm supplies, Fothergill invited the other three men to sail back with him to Wiarton, and, as none were the type to pass up a free ride, they readily agreed. It looked like it was to be a pleasant afternoon.

When Fothergill failed to arrive home his friends formed a search party. They were led to White Cloud Island by the agonized sound of a whimpering dog. On shore they found Fothergill's boat, still full of supplies, and Charles Kennedy's corpse on the nearby sand. The distraught men combed the island, but found only Fothergill's empty pocket book and his personal papers blowing about in the grass. An investigation began midst wild speculation. A notorious outlaw from a well-respected family in Keppel had done it; three known criminals in Owen Sound had done it; one of the men murdered the others and left the area; and so on. The police knew only that the men were missing, and that the last time they were spotted, all four were in Fothergill's boat passing Big Bay, towing a smaller boat. The unearthing of the skeletons thirty years later provided the "where," but the story is still looking for the "why" and "who."

Today, Griffith Island is an exclusive game preserve and private hunting club. It is strictly off-limits to boaters, except in emergency situations. It is also home to one of the six "Imperial Tower" lighthouses constructed between 1855 and 1859 by the Department of Public Works, Canada West.

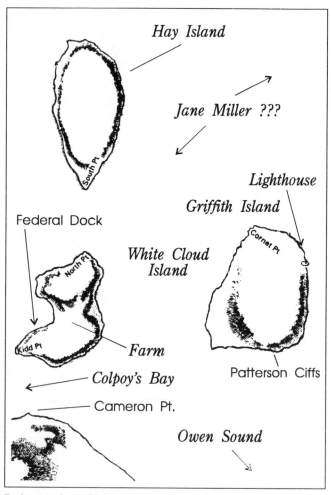

Hay Island

Jane Miller ???

Lighthouse

Griffith Island

Federal Dock

White Cloud Island

North Pt.

Cornet Pt.

Kidd Pt.

Farm

Patterson Ciffs

Colpoy's Bay

Cameron Pt.

Owen Sound

Refer to chart 2282

Hay Island
The Manasoo

When two Hungarian brothers settled on Hay Island in the 1920s they surely didn't think their animals would be their legacy to Georgian Bay. But it is so. Offspring of their European wild boars have been reported roaming free to this day.

The steamer, the *Manasoo*, is believed to have sunk just north of Hay Island. According to James Barry, in *Georgian Bay, An Illustrated History,* the ship was heading down from Manitoulin on September 14, 1928, with 116 head of cattle as part of its cargo. During the night, a storm arose. As the boat rocked violently in the heavy seas, the cattle all shifted to one side, causing the ship to roll over and sink. Sixteen people lost their lives.

Bruce's Caves Conservation Area and the Bruce's Caves

Around the turn of the century, early tourists to these caves were greeted by an eccentric gentleman dressed in ill-fitting pants, a paperbag hat, and a jacket made from flannelette blankets. "The cave hermit" would charge them a small entrance fee and often entertain them with stories told in his soft-spoken voice. His name was Robert Bruce. Originally from Scotland, he came to Georgian Bay to work in the mines. The mine suffered a collapse and trapped Bruce beneath the rubble. The cruel foreman made no effort to rescue him - loudly announcing to just leave him for dead. But Robert Bruce was alive! When eventually unearthed he went after the foreman with a

The Hermit of the Bruce Caves

pickax but luckily was too exhausted to catch him.

Robert lived a rather solitary life in a small cabin near the caves limiting his contact with humans to friendly tourists who came through the area. He died in 1908, his life story relatively unknown, leaving behind as his legacy his name on these breathtaking caves.

Today the conservation area - located three miles northeast of Wiarton, just east of Oxenden - consists of 241 acres (97ha) of hardwood forest and stunningly layered cave formations overlooking Colpoy's Bay. There is no lake access to the caves, but you can see them by taking the Bruce Trail from the parking lot of the conservation area. Along the way are many interesting geological sites ranging from rock crevices and sink holes to boulder beaches.

Wiarton

In 1866, when James Lennox put the last hewn log on his cabin he didn't know he was building on the site of a future town. Two years later, lots starting at $6 were offered for sale and Wiarton began to fan out along the hill. Shoreline residents arrived after the dock was built with a $300 Indian Department grant. Wiarton served as a shipping centre for the Peninsula - transporting lumber and fish, and for a short time beet sugar refined at a Wiarton plant. Unlike so many of the smaller Bay towns, Wiarton survived the decline of both the timber and fishing industries, and has continued as a thriving commercial and manufacturing centre, as well as being home to the Bay's Coast Guard. Its surrounding conservation areas preserve its diverse natural attractions as well as some of its unique, and mysterious history.

City of Chatham Wreck
Okonra Wreck

Neither bad weather nor foul play ended the nearly thirty-five-year career of this trusty passenger vessel. Instead her demise was brought on by a much stronger force on the Bay - progress. The popularity of the car and the proliferation of roads signalled an end to steamer travel. The *City of Chatham,* which could carry 627 passengers and serviced the Great Lakes and St. Mary's River, was one of

Wiarton

many vessels to be unceremoniously stripped and sunk. Although originally thought to be "out of sight, out of mind," these wrecks continue to play an important role in the Bay's marine heritage.

The 136-foot (40.8m) *City of Chatham* - at one time thought to be the wreck of the pioneer steamer *Okonra*, lies very close to shore, just north of the Wiarton fish hatchery. She is opposite a very large boulder sitting on mainland. Swim north from the road running along the shore and snorkel in the blue water until you see the ribs of the wreck lying on the sandy bottom.

The Edward S. Pease and Lothair Wrecks

At the turn of the century, the old lumber barge, The *Edward S. Pease*, and the tired Scottish-built barge, the *Lothair*, were deliberately sunk by a mill company to form a holding pond for logs destined for the adjacent mill.

Both wrecks are located just south of the pier at the hamlet of Colpoy's Bay in about ten to twelve feet (3m to 3.6m) of water. They are partly visible from the surface when the water is low. To distinguish between the two, the *Lothair* is closer to shore and her stern post reaches almost to the surface. This site is perfect for snorkeling and for the novice scuba diver.

Spirit Rock Conservation Area

Located just north of Wiarton, the Spirit Rock Conservation Area is a beautiful 217 acre (87ha) spot with remarkable views of Colpoy's Bay. But its beauty is shadowed by an ancient legend of broken hearts and dreams. A very long time ago, the eastern and western tribes were at war. A young girl from the west was captured and made a slave. Taken by her beauty a young man from the eastern tribe fell in love with the maiden and freed her. Together they escaped into the woods. A search party caught up with them and the punishment for his disloyalty was severe - he was thrown off the cliff. Grief stricken the girl returned to her people, but they rejected her as a traitor. Overwhelmed by despair, she returned to the cliff and threw herself off to join her young lover.

This tragic tale of lost love has been told in nearly every culture in the world. The Spirit Rock legend, however, has a twist that makes it stand apart from Romeo and Juliet. In 1890, W.G. Cheshire and Jim Millar, tired of skating on Colopy's Bay, climbed up the cliff to do some exploring. They found a cave and went inside. Discovering a second tunnel blocked by a boulder the boys pushed the boulder aside. They were shocked to see two skeletons. The coroner later confirmed they were of a man and woman - both were very, very old.

The Corran

Within the Spirit Rock Conservation Area are the ruins of Alexander McNeil's magnificent estate, The Corran, built in 1882. McNeil was a wealthy lawyer, a meticulous and intelligent man who cared deeply for his seventeen-room mansion and its grounds: three acres (1.2ha) of flower gardens, immaculate lawns, and bountiful orchards. For over twenty years McNeill was a federal Member of Parliament. Proud to share his luxurious home, he gave numerous parties, entertaining other MPs and political leaders. As each of the party guests left he would present them with a freshly picked rose from one of his five hundred rose bushes.

When McNeill died at the age of ninety, his son Malcolm took over the estate but with little enthusiasm.

Alexander McNeil

While he squandered the family fortune, his father's life-time passion deteriorated. When Malcolm died in 1956, he left the estate to the family housekeeper of thirty-three years, who in turn sold it to a Toronto resident. After many years of neglect and vandalism all that was left for the Conservation Authority was the burned stone shell of a once grand mansion and some overgrown gardens.

You can get to the site by taking a dinghy to the shore. A marked trail will lead you up the same spiral staircase that McNeil used to enjoy the waters of Colpoy's Bay. By

The rundown Corran in the 1950s

car, drive north of Wiarton on Highway 6 to the Spirit Rock Conservation Area.

The Bruce Trail

If you need to stretch your legs, this is the excursion for you. The Bruce Trail was completed in 1967 and is a 774-km continuous foot path that follows the Niagara Escarpment from Tobermory all the way to Niagara. Archeologists are still uncovering some of the escarpment's hidden treasures: artifacts from the War of 1812; native burial grounds for important shamans and tribal leaders; and human faces carved into the cliffs by aboriginal people. In the *Jesuit Relations,* it is recorded that natives believed souls had to pass through many dangers along the escarpment face in order to reach the villages of the dead. The Bruce Trail is alive with these spirits.

From Tobermory to Wiarton the trail offers spectacular vistas of the white cliffs and turqoise waters. There are rocky beaches, unique flowers and vegetation, and numerous caves carved out of the limestone by the relentless waves. South of Wiarton the trail heads inland and curves around Georgian Bay as far as Craigleith, passing old mills, hamlets, and waterfalls. The escarpment is also home to 36 species of reptiles and amphibians; 53 species of mammals including white-tailed deer, coyote, red fox, porcupine, raccoon and groundhog; and more than 300 species of birds, turkey vultures and hawks among them. Beware the escarpment's other inhabitant, poison ivy. Some sites of interest include Smokey Head where faint traces of log slides remain; Devil's Monument (p.237); and pot-holes (p.233).

If traveling by boat you can dock at Wiarton, Lion's Head, or Tobermory and join the trail there. The main trail is marked by white blazes. Blue and yellow blazes indicate side trails. If interested, obtain a copy of the *Guide to the Bruce Trail,* from the Bruce Trail Association, P.O. Box 857, Hamilton, Ontario, L8N 3N9.

Cape Croker

When their land claims were ignored in the early
1800s (page 210), Indians from the Owen
Sound/Presqu'ile area were coerced into moving to Cape
Croker. This area has served as an Indian reserve ever
since, and is currently the home of more than 600 Ojibwa.
For some time the Cape Croker Indian Band chose to
remain isolated. They developed into a strong, self-contained community under fine leadership. The band prospered in the late 1800s by harvesting and selling, of all
crops, passenger pigeons.

Each year thousands upon thousands of passenger
pigeons migrated through the area. As the stories go, the
sun would be blocked out by the pigeons as they traveled
and nested their way up the Peninsula, picking the area
clean of its berries and peas. They were a favourite target
for hunters, and every spring the land was covered with
feathers and blood. Chicks were sold to the southern markets as squab, while Bruce residents ate mature passenger
pigeon at least once a day during spring and summer.
Early pioneer and author Catherine Parr Traill's recipes
for pigeons in her *Canadian Settler's Guide* include:
roasted pigeon, pigeons in crust and pigeon-pie - "Season
your pigeons well with pepper and salt; as many as will lay
in your pie-dish; dust a little flour on, thin; add a cup of
hot water; cover your pie, and bake an hour. Note -
Pigeons are best for table just after harvest: the young
birds are then very fat."

Despite the passenger pigeons' ability to reproduce
rapidly and in great numbers, the speed and efficiency

with which they were being slaughtered was too great. By 1902, only three pigeons were sighted. The following year, there were none. Like the harvests of fish and forest, the harvest of passenger pigeon was bountiful but short-lived. Today, the occasional flock of gulls circling around the Bay is only a tiny reminder of the great hordes of pigeons that once filled the sky.

Cape Croker Park
Cape Croker Loop Walking Trail

Although Cape Croker is an Indian reserve there is a campground available in Cape Croker Park, on the southeast shore of Sydney Bay under the Jones Bluff. Both Sydney and Hope Bay provide good shelter for mooring, but Sydney Bay is the preferred shelter in rough weather.

The Park also provides access to the beautiful Jones Bluff Loop, a forty-five minute detour to the main Bruce Trail. This route follows an historic Indian walking trail, with cliff look-outs over Georgian Bay, limestone terraces, meadows with wild grape vines, and mature hardwood forests. The Chippewa of Newash Band have given the Bruce hikers permission to pass through the reserve. If leaving a car, either ask permission, or put a note on the windshield explaining that you are a hiker. The trail begins at the parking lot of the old store once run by Joe and Irene Akiwenzie, whose stories often entertained hikers lucky enough to meet them.

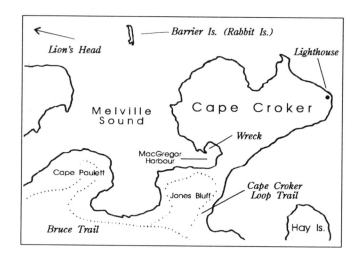

Refer to chart 2282

The J.H. Jones Mystery

J.V. Crawford concentrated heavily as he maneuvered the 125-foot (37.5m) freight tug, *J.H. Jones*, through 25-foot (7.5m) waves. He was making his final trip of the season, loaded down with machinery and bricks from Wiarton. The *J.H. Jones* pulled into Owen Sound for one last pickup before making her way to Lion's Head and up to Manitoulin Island. Tension among the twelve-member crew was high as they carried barrels of coal oil onto the back of the tug. Everyone knew she was already over-

J.H. Jones

loaded. Someone said, "You know the *Waubuno* went down this day about forty-nine years ago." No one responded. No one even looked up. While lashing the barrels together, the crew eyed the seventeen passengers boarding the ship. As they pulled out of the harbour, the passenger, Alex Lyons, lifted the somber mood briefly with wild tales of his recent trip to the Yukon goldrush. Lyons stopped mid-story - his audience focused on the waves that were now pounding over the bow. Captain Crawford didn't move his intense gaze from the churning waters.

Mrs. Crawford opened the front door to see her neighbour huddled behind his black raincoat on the stoop. Taking off his drenched hat, he greeted the Crawford's six children sitting silently around the kitchen table. "It's still blow'n like mad, but they say she'll be lett'n up by Saturday." He was wrong. The storm raged for days and a search crew could not be dispatched until Monday morning - four days after the *J.H. Jones* was last seen by Captain William Chapman from the Cape Croker Lighthouse.

On Monday the search crew found nothing. On Tuesday, people from Penetang and Collingwood joined the search. By Wednesday, everyone knew the answer. Chief Montague on Christian Island came across two lifeboats bearing the *J.H. Jones'* name among pieces of the wreck that were strewn along the beach. People now focused on recovering the dead. But none were found. Winter came without mercy, and the town of Wiarton raised one thousand dollars for the suffering widows and their children. People prayed that in the spring, the hull, and maybe some of the bodies, would be recovered. A funeral might relieve the suffering of the community. But nothing was found. They had vanished.

Three years after the community began to heal, the Bay spat up a ghastly reminder of her power. A fisherman walking along the shore of Cape Croker came across two barrels, the metal worn smooth by the waves - two barrels of coal oil. Everyone has a theory on where the *J. H. Jones* can be found. Cape Croker Fisherman say she is at the mouth of the Bay where their nets snag something in about 100 feet (30m) of water. Only the Bay and the *J.H. Jones* know the answer.

Barrier Island/Rabbit Island

On Barrier Island the Ojibwa used to set up lake trout camps each fall. They called it Rabbit Island because of the large numbers of rabbits found there. This changed when some Lion's Head residents had a contest in 1936 in which every rabbit was shot and left in piles on the beach to rot.

Lion's Head
Lion's Head Provincial Nature Reserve - Potholes

Approaching from the south, a profile of a lion emerges from the overhanging bluff about two miles (3.2km) northeast of the actual village of Lion's Head. Lion's Head, like so many other Georgian Bay towns was born during the lumber boom in the late 1870s and served as a key port in the Bruce lumber trade. And, following the formula, when the lumber supply dwindled, Lion's Head turned to tourism for sustenance.

Today, the development of Lion's Head Provincial Nature Reserve and the spectacular hiking trails along the Bruce Trail attract a steady flow of tourists to the area, as well as regular boating traffic from up and down the peninsula. The 1,315-acre (526-ha) Reserve, near the village of Lion's Head, preserves the greatest concentration of potholes in the province. There are hundreds of them on the 100-foot (30m) cliffs of the Niagara Escarpment.

Two theories exist about how these potholes came to be. Conventional thought suggests they were formed by

Lion's Head

the melt waters from the retreating ice age glaciers flowing into cracks in the rock. Over time, both water and rocks ground out bigger and bigger holes in the soft limestone. A more controversial hypothesis suggests these potholes were formed by highly pressurized water in a very short period of time - possibly hours. As melt water collected in the rock, the weight and pressure of the ice caused the water to explode at weak spots. This pressurized water burst with enough force to carve the solid rock into incredible shapes. It is suggested that the profusion of potholes was the result of melt water rushing southwest along the bottom of Georgian Bay. When it hit promontories such as Lion's Head, it split into two streams powerful enough to sculpt the potholes. One pothole is over thirteen feet (4m) deep and almost six feet (2m) wide. Standing inside this giant tube, you can feel a low rumbling of energy and power, and hear the rushing of great waters.

To get to the potholes, follow the road into Lion's Head village. Take Moore Street past the High School until cottages are spotted on the left and open fields on the right. Look for the entrance to a bush road on the right, with Bruce Trail white blazes. It takes about twenty minutes to reach the top of the cliffs and the potholes. The big chimney pothole is marked by a double blaze. The entrance hole is located in a cliff to the right. To see more potholes, visit the Hope Bay Forest Provincial Nature Reserve further south.

The 26-mile (16km) trail around the Lion's Head peninsula offers a stunning view of the Bay's turquoise water and surrounding cliffs. The spectacular hike follows a fairly untraveled path. On sunny days, large fish can be seen swimming near the rocks in the Bay hundreds of feet below. For complete information on the Bruce Trail, consult the *Guide to the Bruce Trail* put out by the Bruce Trail Association (P.O. Box 857, Hamilton, Ontario L8N 3N9.)

NOTE: This hike should only be attempted in good weather as the trail hugs the cliffs of the escarpment, sometimes only inches from the edge. In inclement weather, the flat limestone can be slippery. Poison ivy is everywhere.

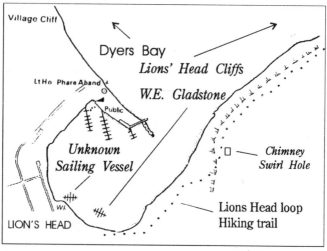

Refer to chart 2282

Lion's Head Wrecks
Unknown and the W.E. Gladstone Wrecks

The Bay's unpredictable weather cannot take credit for all the shipwrecks lost in its murky depths. Many are intentionally sunk when they no longer prove sea-worthy. An area just southeast of the village of Lion's Head has served as a "dumping ground" for many of these vessels over the years; the marine equivalent to an auto graveyard. This area, filled with burned, worn hulls, cribs, and other marine debris, is a diver's and snorkeler's dream.

There are two relatively intact wrecks to be found. One appears to be a sailing vessel used in the lumber trade. It is about 140 feet (42m) long and was probably abandoned due to old age. Further to the east lies the remains of the tugboat *W.E. Gladstone,* sunk in November 1908 after many years of service.

Both wrecks are fairly easy to find. The unknown sailing ship rests in shallow water with its bow up against the shore of a small peninsula southeast of Lion's Head public beach. The *Gladstone* lies further east about 200 feet (60m) offshore in 15 feet (4.5m) of water. Both the wrecks and the surrounding area are excellent sites for divers or snorkelers. *NOTE: Beware of heavy boat traffic.*

Devil's Monument
Devil's Face

Dyer's Bay offers some breathtaking sights, whether traveling by foot or flipper. One of the oldest and largest flowerpot formations on land, Devil's Monument is located along the Bruce Trail, between Cape Chin and Dyer's Bay. Formed some 5,500 years ago by the wave action of glacial Lake Nipissing, the monument stands between the Escarpment and the shoreline. A staircase and a blue-blazed side trail lead down the Escarpment to the base of the flowerpot. There is an interpretive display at the site.

Further north, other impressive rock formations can be found above and below water. Devil's Face, located one mile (1.6km) south of Dyer's Bay, offers an intriguing configuration of rocks and boulders, canyon-like passages, nooks, crannies, cliffs, caves, and unique marine life for both the diver and snorkeler to explore. *NOTE: It is easy to be lured too deep by all the spectacular surroundings.*

If looking for further diving opportunities on Dyer's Bay check out the Dyer's Bay anchor located off the Dyer Bayside Resort (the site is usually marked with a jug.) The large fluked anchor is in 40 feet (12m) of water, and is now used as a diver training site.

The Mystery Of Ghost Lake Mill
Gillies Lake

Horace Lymburner and his son Robert saw nothing but potential when the captain of the *Jane Miller* (p.212) showed them the shores south of Cabot Head in 1881. On the cliff 200 feet (60m) above the beach, there were plenty of trees, and for any lumbermen the added bonus of a lake with a stream pouring down the cliff to carry logs. Be damned with the Indian legend of a Ghost Lake curse.

Ghost Lake, or Gillies Lake as it is now called, earned its reputation from an incident involving Indians who once lived along its shores. One disastrous winter day, many of the villagers were ice fishing for trout. A great cracking sound filled the cold air. In a matter of seconds, the huge solid sheet of ice shattered into hundreds of floes. Only six people survived. The remaining members of the village decided to leave the spot and never came back.

Lymburner agreed the lake was undeniably ghostly. Viewed from above, the shallow end of the lake with its chalk-white limestone floor looked like a white porcelain

Ghost Lake mill

moon among the trees. Lining the shore, and covering aquatic plants was a thick coat of "whitewash." Even tiny mollusks were white. The fish in the deeper part of the lake had an alarming pallor, with bellies, sides, fins, and flesh ghoulishly white. Locals called them "mountain trout," a mutated species unknown in other lakes.

The Lymburners constructed their operation on the narrow beach. Cut logs were sent indiscriminately over the precipice and formed tangled heaps on the jagged limestone below. So mutilated by the fall, many logs were good only for fuel. During the winter, the pile of logs froze solidly and did not thaw out until mid-summer. Not to mention the dangerous job of prying the giant logs from

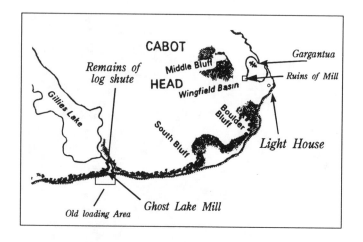

Refer to chart 2282

the mountainous pile towering above — pick-up-sticks it was not. It was obvious changes had to be made. A basin was dug on the shore then an inclined trench was carved out from the lake. From this trench a wooden flume was built down the cliff face - making a much more efficient way to control the lumber from above. The Ghost Lake Mill was in operation.

At its peak, 12,000 board-lumber feet were cut a day - impressive for such a small mill. The mill continued to prosper until the northern tip of the Bruce Peninsula was practically bare of trees. In 1905, after twenty-five years, Lymburner's mill was closed. Except for the odd incident they thought they had escaped the curse of the lake.

Others might have disagreed.

While the Lymburners were not affected directly, the curse affected others associated with the mill. On her last trip before sinking to her mysterious grave in November 1881 the *Jane Miller* (p. 212) delivered equipment to the Lymburner mill site. The *Nellie Sherwood,* full of the mill's first two shipments of shingles and lumber, sank right in front of the mill in the great storm of September 1882, the same storm which took down the *Asia* (see page 140) and numerous other vessels. A third mishap struck a young sawyer who mysteriously drowned in Ghost Lake.

The mill site is located along the southern shore of Cabot Head and can be accessed by water and car. The cliff is slightly barren where the log-chute was - only faint traces of it remain. The fastest way to confirm the site is to walk up the cliff to the lake. Follow its shores to the place where Lymburner cut a V shape in the shoreline. This is where the chute was once attached. Today the water pours through the cut, forms a small stream then vanishes underground. If you put your ear to the ground you can hear the water rushing underneath. Straight down the hill are remnants of Lymburners ingenious flume rotting on the ground.

Cabot Head
Wingfield Basin

On the heel of the Bruce Peninsula, there once was a fishing harbour and small mill. Today a pile of rotting timber on the shore is the only clue. Wingfield Basin was used as a collection depot for wood to be later cut into square timber. When the mill shut down the Basin became a pleasant refuge for boats and fishing tugs. The *Gargantua* took quite a shining to it too.

The Gargantua Shipwreck

Bound for the North Channel, a tug laboured through the rolling November seas towing a worn 318-ton wooden steam tug, the *Gargantua*. In 1952 after many distinguished years of service the *Gargantua* was stripped of her machinery and like other ships of her age and class was slated to spend her final days as a lumber barge.

 This was not to be. The *Gargantua* sprang a leak near Cabot Head. The captain ordered the crew to save her by towing her into the shallows. The crew unceremoniously dumped the *Gargantua* in Wingfield Basin. Her owners promised to return the following spring to remove her, but as the ice floes departed and summer came, the *Gargantua* still lay in Wingfield Basin's tranquil waters. Knowing how strained the hull was, her owners had no intention of raising her. Grass and shrubs took root among her planks and locals became accustomed to her silhouette. In 1971 an unexplained fire ravaged her decks.

Much of the *Gargantua* can still be seen intact above water. Her hull goes down 15 feet (4.5m). *NOTE: Visibility is often limited because of heavy silt. At times boat traffic can be quite heavy.*

Posing for the camera

As we left Wingfield Basin in the early morning, the sun's low angle threw dramatic shafts of light through her exposed ribs, reminding us that we were about to enter the Graveyard of Georgian Bay.

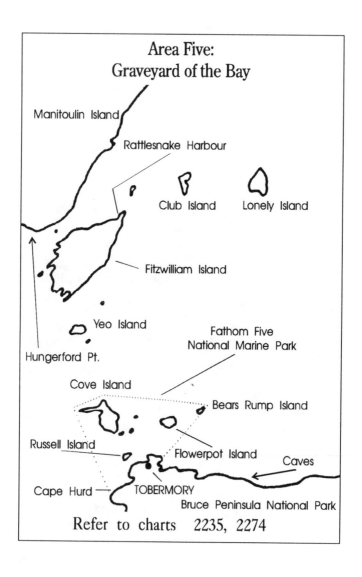

Area Five:
Graveyard of the Bay

Manitoulin Island

Rattlesnake Harbour

Club Island

Lonely Island

Fitzwilliam Island

Yeo Island

Fathom Five
National Marine Park

Hungerford Pt.

Cove Island

Bears Rump Island

Russell Island

Flowerpot Island

Caves

Cape Hurd

TOBERMORY

Bruce Peninsula National Park

Refer to charts   2235, 2274

5

Graveyard of the Bay:
Cabot Head to Manitoulin Island

Something in this area makes you peer into the deep water, catching sight of a dark shape below - or was it a trick of the light? Something in this area makes you scan the tall, jagged cliffs of the escarpment, searching through its woods for a glimpse of... what? Perhaps you are responding to the combined energies of the phantom hermits, the benevolent keeper of the light, the Great Spirit, Kitchikewana, and all the souls that have been lost to this area, now calling out for recognition. For below this region's exterior beauty and obvious recreational opportunities lies something darker, more intriguing. This area is "the Graveyard of the Bay," and this is how it earned its title.

Beginning in the early 1860s, the region from

Pathfinder on Georgian Bay

Tobermory to the southernmost tip of Fitzwilliam Island was a key trade and transportation route to Lake Huron. If the weather co-operated it was relatively safe. The odds decreased when it was dark, windy, rainy, or worse, snowing. Over the years, many vessels have foundered along the passage.

In 1971, the area known historically as the Cape Hurd Islands was recognized as a valuable heritage site and designated a national marine park. Today, Fathom Five National Marine Park is the first and only underwater park in North America intended to protect, preserve, and educate the public about, our marine heritage and aquatic resources. Within its boundaries it contains twenty-one known sail and steam wrecks and numerous other dive sites of geological interest, offering opportunities for all levels of diver (and snorkeler.)

This chapter is necessarily heavy with dive sites and how-to-find tips, but there is much to explore above water as well.

Bruce Peninsula National Park
Underwater Caves

Travelling northwest around Cabot Head along the shores of the Bruce Peninsula National Park, the visitor is met by one of the most breathtaking views on the Peninsula. From the rugged limestone profile of the escarpment's streaked cliffs to the mysterious deep caves harbouring hermit ghosts, swallows, bats, and other den-dwelling creatures; from the thick woodlands fronted by great stretches of white pebble beaches to the sparkling blue-green mirror of water, this park has much to see and photograph.

The park offers 242 campsites within its three campgrounds and has direct access to the top section of the Bruce Trail, which winds through both private and public land containing forests, swamps, beaches, cliffs and caves. (And mosquitoes, flies, and poison ivy!) For information, contact: Bruce Peninsula National Park, P.O. Box 189, Tobermory, Ont., N0H 2R0. Telephone: (519) 596-2233.

Our first ghost awaits just north of Halfway Rock Point, along the cliffs of Cyprus Lake Provincial Park, 10

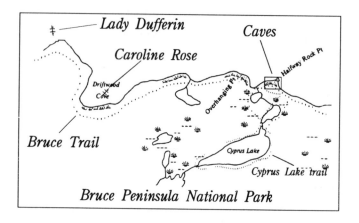

Refer to chart 2235

miles (16km) east of Tobermory. Submerged caves lead
from the open waters of the Bay to a grotto where, long
ago, a local hermit would come for his weekly bath. Stand
quietly in the entrance to this grotto, and hear the splash
of the water as the hermit rinses off the suds.

The best approach is by boat. Travel north around
Halfway Rock Point to the entrance of a big cave. If diving, enter one of two submerged entrances a bit further
south and follow 16 to 20 foot (5 to 6m) passageways into
the grotto. If on foot, follow the rugged one-mile (1.5km)
path to the grotto. Once inside the limestone vault, the
water is illuminated by the underwater tunnel to the Bay.
Don't forget to listen for the hermit.

Lady Dufferin Wreck
Caroline Rose Wreck

It was just another job for the steamer *W.B. Hall.* With the *Lady Dufferin*, a tired old 135-foot (40.5-m) schooner in tow, it set out one October day in 1886 to rescue a load of lumber from a grounded schooner, the John Bentley. With the cargo transferred to the *Lady Dufferin*, the *W.B. Hall* began the slow laboured tow back to Tobermory. Black clouds rolled in and the wind picked up. Soon a strong October gale was tossing both vessels around. The tow line broke. The *W.B. Hall* could do nothing for the helpless crew of the *Lady Dufferin*, as she was swept into the rocks east of Driftwood Cove. Fortunately, her crew escaped, but had to watch as the ship broke up and sank.

The *Lady Dufferin* can be found in about 70 feet (21m) of cold water. Swimming over her broken hull, the darkness of the Bay seems to close in. The site is found southeast of Tobermory, just off the point between Driftwood Cove and Little Cove. At the location, there is a notch in the rock with two small white circles painted below.

Built in 1940 by the same Lunenburg company that built the *Bluenose*, the *Caroline Rose* was one of the last Grand Bank schooners to be used for fishing. Her next incarnation was as a cruise ship but after sinking at the dock in Owen Sound, she was towed to the area around the *Lady Dufferin* and purposely sunk as a dive site. But the Bay, angry at this infringement of what she considered to be her job, had the last say. In the fall of 1990, a severe Bay storm lifted the 250-ton ship right off the lake floor and deposited her 100 feet (30m) away, smashing her badly in the process.

Many of the ship's original fittings can still be found, along with her engine, pipes, nozzles, tools, propeller and smoke stack. The hull has caved in, and thanks to the storm, pieces are scattered over a wide area. The best way to find the site is to anchor in the middle of Driftwood Cove. The buoy marks a rope which leads down through the 60 feet (18m) of blackness to the broken hull.

NOTE: *This dive is quite deep and the water can be cold, so take extra care.*

Tobermory
Fathom Five National Marine Park

Poor soil, thick forests, murky swamps, and plenty of water greeted Tobermory's first settlers (at the time the town was called Collins Harbour.) Added to this were the hazards of fires, drought and long periods of isolation. Yet the settlers came. Unable to cultivate anything much more than rocks, early residents turned to lumbering and fishing.

By the 1860s, it was turning a tidy profit as a lumber port, supporting three sawmills. Blessed with two excellent natural harbours - Big Tub and Little Tub - it quickly became the trade and transportation centre for the Peninsula. By the mid-1880s, it had also established itself as a thriving commercial fishing village, servicing fishermen from Goderich, Southampton, and Meaford, who

Tobermory fishermen mending nets

set up fishing stations on the harbour's surrounding islands. It was one of these Goderich fishermen, a home-sick Scot originally from the Isle of Mull, who wanted to rename Collins Harbour "Tobermory" because it remind-ed him so much of his Hebridean harbour village. Without much protest, the village was renamed.

Following the pattern of Bay industries, the lumber business slowed as the timber supply dwindled. Fortunately, commercial fishing was booming, and became the mainstay of Tobermory's economy. By 1930, 15 steam tugs were hauling fish. That same year, the steam tugs were joined in the harbour by the first ferry from Tobermory to Manitoulin Island. The 90-foot (27-m) long

30 pound trout at Tobermory

Kagawong could take eight cars on its daily trip. (Today's 365-foot (109.5-m), 140-car *Chi-Cheemaun* runs three to four times daily during the spring and summer.)

Beginning in 1855, major navigational aids - mainly lighthouses - were built on Georgian Bay to serve the heavy marine traffic. Some early models were a little more primitive. When John Charles Earl settled at the mouth of Big Tub harbour, he hung a lantern at the harbour's entrance thus becoming the first unofficial light keeper on the Bay. Captains relied so heavily on Earl's light, that they gave him some of their cargo in gratitude. In 1885, a "real" lighthouse was erected in Big Tub harbour, and John Charles Earl became Big Tub's official light keeper. One year later, the Cove Island lighthouse was built and, in 1887, a third on Flowerpot Island was erected.

The increased number of lighthouses along this treacherous stretch failed to prevent all shipwrecks. An archipelago of shoals and reefs, of strong currents and winds have made this Main Channel one of the Bay's most perilous passages. It is an ongoing game of chance. Many seasons pass with no losses, then, in a violent rage, the Bay will scoop up a handful of ships and pull them to the bottom.

Isolated for years, many wrecks are now part of Fathom Five National Marine Park, providing an opportunity to explore the past. These powerful memorials invoke the exciting period in Canadian marine history when the Bay was dotted with sails, paddle wheels, and smokestacks. Within this 29,137-acre (11,655-ha) park, much can be learned about nineteenth and twentieth-century sail and steam vessels. Encompassing 19 islands - Cove, Echo, North and South Otter, Russel, Bear's Rump, Middle, Flowerpot and a few smaller islands - and the Tobermory shores, the park contains 21 known wrecks (most of which are discussed below.) It is believed many more await discovery. If diving in this area, abide by park rules and carry charts showing locations of the wrecks.

For those not diving or snorkeling, spend a day or two exploring the Bruce Trail, visiting the St. Edmunds Township Museum or other historic attractions along the harbour, catching a nature or diving film at the Crow's Nest Theatre, or taking a ferry over to Flowerpot Island.

Little Tub Harbour
John & Alex Wreck, Robert K. Wreck
Alice G. Wreck and Bob Foote Wreck

After battling the Bay's winds and waves for a combined thirty-one years of service, the *John & Alex* tug and the *Robert K.* tug deserved to retire with dignity. Unfortunately, being destroyed by fire while safely docked in Little Tub Harbour was not very dignified. The 60-foot (18-m) *John & Alex,* in the Tobermory fishing fleet for 13 years, caught fire in the early morning of December 6, 1947. A threat to the vessels around her, she was towed to the harbour's mouth where she burned to the waterline and sank. The 68-foot (20.4m) *Robert K.*, a well-known fishing boat that serviced the area for 18 years, was also destroyed by fire June 23, 1935.

The remains of *John & Alex*'s stern-tube, engine-bed and concrete ballast lie with the 50-foot (15-m) long section of her hull, just east of the entrance to the harbour. Her stern is just discernible, and the bow is in about 15 feet (4.5 m) of water. A bit east, in slightly deeper water are parts of her sides and keel. A less entertaining dive, the *Robert K.* is closer to shore, directly off the shoreline access in front of the motel. A piece of her stern and port lies alongside a 55-foot (16.5-m) long section of the hull. Both provide a safe training ground for those just getting their "diving legs."

The *Alice G. tug*, another dependable fishing vessel was yanked from her mooring in 1927 by gale-force

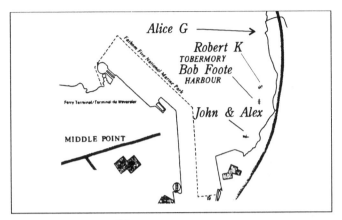

Refer to chart 2274

November winds and run aground against the broken shore below the harbour's North Point. Because she was not ravaged by fire, the *Alice G.* is perhaps the most interesting, intact wreck in the harbour. She offers a clear view not only of her drive shaft, propeller, boiler, and steam engine, but also of the graceful curve of her railing. The *Alice G.* keeps the *Robert K.* company, lying about 100 yards (90 m) north in 20 feet (6 m) of water.

Tugs were the "oxen" of the Bay. Their sturdy hulls and powerful engines enabled them to perform the vital tasks of towing lumber barges and log booms, delivering fish, and ice-breaking. When the *Bob Foote* tug was completely spent she was sent to her watery grave in 1902. She lies southwest of the *Robert K.* in 20 to 25 feet (6 to 7.5 m) of water. Her sides have collapsed and her deck has fallen through. Just west of the Bob Foote are the remains of two wooden cribs. *Note: All four wrecks are easy to find, and are marked with boating buoys. A divers' platform rests above the wrecks. Watch for boating traffic.*

Big Tub Harbour
Sweepstakes Wreck

It was another swift and undignified retirement - the victim a popular two-masted schooner, the *Sweepstakes*. Built in 1867, this 130-foot (39-m) vessel serviced the area for almost twenty years. She now makes an interesting dive site, as she is one of the better preserved nineteenth-century schooners in the area. In August 1885, the *Sweepstakes* was run aground and damaged on Cove Island (see Cove Island story.) A salvage crew freed her, but while being towed to Big Tub for repairs, she sank.

A mooring buoy lies just east of this wreck. The almost-intact hull is about 50 yards (45m) from the end of Big Tub Harbour in 20 feet (7m) of water. A far-more interesting wreck than the ones in Little Tub, the Sweepstakes still feels like a schooner. Its starboard railing is intact and her windlass and winch can be seen. Holes two-feet in diameter through the deck give an idea of the size and location of the masts. Her cargo hatches are open, but, for safety and preservation reasons, do not enter, as tempting as it may seem.

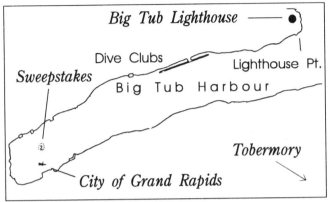

Refer to chart 2274

City of Grand Rapids Wreck

The *City of Grand Rapids* was built in 1879 to replace the ill-fated *J.H. Jones* (see chapter four.) One cold October evening in 1907, her startled crew was roused from sleep by the pungent smell of smoke. By the time they managed to jump to the wharf, smoke was billowing through the windows. An owner of a nearby tug heard the shouting, and pulled the steamer away from the dock before the dock could ignite. However, the inferno forced the tug to release her and the 122-foot (36.6-m) steamer drifted slowly back into Big Tug Harbour, lighting the night sky.

The *City of Grand Rapids* sank about 100 feet (30m) off the *Sweepstakes*' bow in shallow water. Her propeller and rudder were recovered by an early salvage team and are now on display at the St. Edmunds Township

City of Grand Rapids

Museum. Along with her intact hull, a steam engine crank-shaft, parts of her boiler, propeller shaft and shaft coupling remain. NOTE: *These sites have a regulated diving and snorkeling schedule in conjunction with the glass-bottomed tourist boats that visit the sites. Before diving or snorkeling, check the times. Heavy boating traffic is a hazard, and underwater visibility can be a problem because of the sheer number of divers at this site.*

Avalon Voyager II, China, and Cascaden Wrecks

Less notable but worth mentioning are: a 1947 motor-

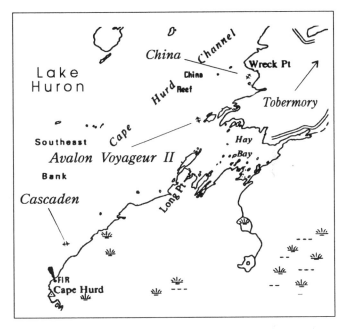

Refer to Charts 2335, 2274

powered vessel slated for a profitable future as a floating restaurant; and two "grunt" schooners from the mid 1880s. The *Avalon Voyager II* was stranded south of China Reef in 15 feet (4.5m) of water in October 1980 after catching fire. Plans for her future as a floating restaurant sank as quickly as she did. The only portion that remains makes a good shallow dive site.

The *China*, built in 1863 and used as a bulk carrier to

haul coal, grain, corn and wood, was trying to make her way through a raging November snowstorm in 1883 when she struck what is now known as China Reef. Salvagers stripped her and the wind and water finished the job, scattering her remains along the reef. This once sturdy 137-foot (41.1-m) schooner lies in 10 feet (3m) of water. Little is known about the schooner, the *Cascaden*, other than she was built in 1866, wrecked in October 1871, and now lies in 20 feet (6m) of water.

John Walters Wreck

Many have speculated that it was one of the Bay's cruel, late autumn storms that added the *John Walters* to her lake bottom schooner collection. In October 1899, while trying to cross the shoal-lined Cape Hurd Channel, this 176-ton, two-masted schooner sank, ending half a century of labour on the Bay. The *John Walters* provides an excellent snorkeling site. We were able to see her hull stretching for quite a distance in the clear water. A small section of the starboard is also visible along with the rudder and centreboard box. This sheltered site is ideal for an easy, relaxing swim.

The hull lies in 10 to 15 feet (3 to 4.5m) of water, just off the south point of Russel Island between the island and a shoal. The bow is located nearer the shore. The rudder can be seen closer to the stern of the wreck. Part of the port side can be found 80 feet (24m) west. *NOTE: Rough waves and hazardous shoals.*

W.L. Wetmore Wreck
James C. King Wreck

Georgian Bay's recipe for a shipping disaster: blowing snow, choppy seas, a heavy load, and in one instance, a channel named after the devil. This lethal combination destroyed both the *W.L. Wetmore*, a 214-foot (64.2m) steamer, and the *James C. King*, a 175-foot (52.5-m) schooner. In the early morning of November 29, 1901, the *W.L. Wetmore* was towing the schooner barges *Brunette* and the *James C. King* loaded with lumber through the

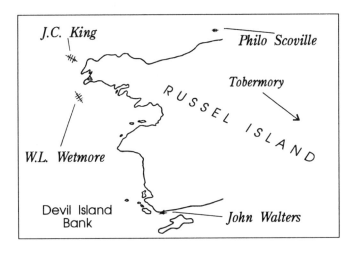

Refer to charts 2235, 2274

W.L. Wetmore

Devil Island Channel to Lake Huron. Impaired visibility forced the *Wetmore* and its tow to run aground on Russel Reef. The violent impact sheared off the *Wetmore*'s 15-foot (4.5m) propeller. As the wild seas ground the *Wetmore* against the rocks, her terrified crew waited and prayed. At dawn they launched a lifeboat and battled the seas to Tobermory. Over the following 24 hours, the waves beat against the *Wetmore*, tearing her massive hull to pieces. The *King* was more fortunate as the waves loosened her position and she slid into deeper water. By the time two tugs arrived from Tobermory the next day, however, only the *Brunette* could be salvaged.

In her time, the *W.L. Wetmore*, built in 1871, was considered one of the finer vessels on the Bay. She is now considered one of the best wrecks in the park. She lies in over 20 feet (6m) of water, just south of the western tip of Russel Island. Two buoys just south and west of the wreck mark her location. If the weather is calm, the exposed boiler is visible. This is an excellent diving site which includes the *Wetmore's* oak rudder, the propeller, her striking boilers, and her bow anchor chains that lead to her large anchor. The site also includes pipes, railings, planking, other iron works, and machinery. It is a popular spot for fish as well.

A mooring buoy indicates the location of the *James C. King,* built in 1867, and now resting on a steep, rocky incline. Her bow is in about 20 feet (6m), and her stern in 90 feet (27m) of water. At 22 feet (6.6m), her rudder and steering gear can be found. Her hull has been split. A large section of the *King's* side and railing is west of the main wreck in 25 feet (7.5m) of water. *NOTE: Swift currents, great depths, and unpredictable weather can be hazards.*

Philo Scoville Wreck

The storm was serious and the location did not help. The gale whipped through Devil's Island Channel and for Captain John O'Gradey, it was like trying to navigate a cork. He ordered the anchors dropped, but they did not catch and dragged uselessly. The *Philo* was on a collision course. Waves whipped over the bow as the 139-foot (41.7-m) long schooner slammed into the north shore of Russel

Island. Stranded on the rocks, she broke up and sank. The crew managed to escape and were later rescued by a tug from Tobermory. Sadly the captain had slipped between the ship and some rocks, and fallen to his death. What is left of the *Philo Scoville* lies on a steep incline off the north shore of Russel Island in 30 to 95 feet (9m to 28.5 m) of water. The anchor can be found to the east of the wreck.

The Griffon Mystery

Although Fathom Five's official list does not include the *Griffon*, there was once evidence that this ship, the first to sail on Georgian Bay, was to be found off Russel Island. As the Bay's first shipwreck, this intriguing story deserves to be told, no matter where she lies.

In 1679, French explorer and trader, Robert-Cavelier Sieur de LaSalle, commissioned the building of the *Griffon*, the first full-sized ship designed specifically for the Great Lakes. LaSalle sent the *Griffon*, piled high with furs, and her six-member crew, including one seven-foot navigator, "Luke the Dane", off to Buffalo on a trading expedition. He would never see the crew or the Griffon again. To this day, divers still search for her unique outline in the water. As described by James Barry in *The Sixth Great Lake,* it was a "high-sterned, square-rigged, three-masted galleon, probably seventy feet long and weighing forty-five tons."

In the late 1880s, a Missisagi Lighthouse keeper and his assistant stumbled across five skeletons in a shoreline

LaSalle's Griffon

cave on Manitoulin Island. They were sure they had found the missing *Griffon* crew. One of the skeletons was so large it could belong to none other than "Luke the Dane." Further searches turned up an ancient wreck resting on a shoal in Missisagi Straits in northern Lake Huron. For years, people referred to it as the "old wreck of the *Griffon*," even though it had been so picked over there was nothing left from which to identify it. Several years ago, a storm pushed it even deeper, closing the door on its identity.

Tobermory commercial fisherman Orrie Vail claimed to have found the real *Griffon* in a shallow cove on Russel Island. It was a spot where his father had said ancient timbers from a seventeenth-century vessel could be found. What Vail uncovered was not much of a vessel but he painstakingly removed a piece and sent it for testing. Results from each of these wrecks indicates the ships were at least 300 years old, but neither has been confirmed as the *Griffon*.

Newaygo Wreck

When the outline of an approaching tug was spied through the blinding snow, tension eased among the crew of the two vessels stranded on the Northwest Bank in MacGregor Channel. The *Newaygo*, a 196-foot (58.8-m) steamer built in 1890, and the *Checotah*, a schooner barge, were caught in a heavy snowstorm that November of 1903. Both vessels were stuck on the southeast rim of the treacherous bank of rocks southwest of Cove Island. Rescue was in sight. But the tug could tow only one vessel. The *Checotah* was chosen, the *Newaygo* was sacrificed. Winter came, and the December waves broke and scattered her remains.

This is a difficult site to locate because of its distance from shore and the lack of convenient landmarks. Use a chart and try to line up the site between the west tip of Cove Island (Gat Point) and Devil Island in the South. It is well worth the search to feel the eerie and somewhat menacing atmosphere of this isolated wreck. Found in less than 20 feet (6m) of water, there is much to explore among its big beams, steel implements, machinery and checkerboard gridwork. *NOTE: Isolation and unpredictable weather are to be considered when diving here.*

Newaygo

Another wreck located between the *Newaygo* and Cove Island is the *Points West*. This wreck is upright and intact in about 50 feet (15m) of water, just east of Harbour Island. It was a wooden tour boat built in Tobermory in 1956, and was scuttled in 1984.

Charles P. Minch Wreck

The captain of the *Charles P. Minch* thought he made the wisest decision the night of October 26, 1898. In fact, it was the only decision he could make when faced with a turbulent southwest gale. The three-masted American

Refer to charts 2235, 2274

schooner found shelter and waited between Echo and Cove Islands for the storm to pass. Suddenly, the wind changed direction and the schooner was thrown into a spin. Her anchor dragged, and she ran aground on the east point of Cove Island's Tecumseh Cove. The shaken yet thankful captain and crew managed to guide themselves to shore by tying a line to a large timber which the waves swept onto the rocky beach. They were safe after struggling through the forest to the lighthouse but the *Charles P. Minch* had already split in two; it was a total loss.

This wreck is a fabulous dive. The curved beamed structure studded with spikes stands in clear water. Two markers indicate the two halves of the wreck. The main portions are found down a rocky slope, near the head of the cove, in 15 to 50 feet (4.5 to 15 m) of water. Just west of the markers there is a rudder which may have belonged to the schooner *Tecumseh*, wrecked in 1882.

Cove Island Lighthouse
The Ghost of Captain Tripp

There is something in the lonely isolated world of a lighthouse keeper and the drafty damp tower he tends that makes one believe this is a world inhabited by ghosts. To the men that kept the light on Cove Island it was the real thing.

Captain Tripp, a sailor of sterling reputation, was in command of the *Regina*, a small schooner whose fresh paint could not hide her years. The term "coffin-ship" was

Cove Island Lighthouse

often used but Captain Tripp had faith in his trusty vessel. It was a clear day in September 1881, when he loaded his cargo at the Goderich dock and headed into the Bay. He had made only one mistake. Instead of picking up a load of lumber, he chose salt.

All was well until the plucky *Regina* rounded Cape Hurd and was hit by a squall. Waves crashed over the bow, adding more water to an already leaky hull. And there was lots to soak it up - lots of salt. With her weight increased a hundred fold by the wet cargo, the relentless pounding of the waves strained her hull. Water seeped even faster through the noticeable gaps in her seams, and the salt continued to drink it up. The *Regina* rode lower and lower in the water but the optimistic Captain believed they could reach a sandbar that was located just off Cove Island. His crew was skeptical, in fact, at this point, they were mutinous. They abandoned ship in a lifeboat and rowed ashore. The ever-faithful Captain Tripp stayed on board, attempting to single-handedly manoeuver his poor *Regina* to safety.

Later questioned about the mutiny the crew's stories were so exaggerated and so contradictory that a full-scale investigation was called. A final evaluation of the wreck which lay near Cove Island, its mast above water, proved both vessel and captain could have been saved had she been kept afloat for a few more minutes. Captain Tripp's body was never found but a rumour circulated that someone had buried him on Cove Island.

On a cold November, years later, the sky turned grey and a storm settled in. Captains strained to see the familiar blink from the Cove Island light through the snow, but it was not there. Panic set in on the water. Suddenly the light reappeared - throwing its welcome beacon. When the keeper was questioned, he admitted the kerosene lamp had gone out. A decade later he confessed more - he was off the island when the incident occurred and the island was completely abandoned. The keeper had always felt a strange presence and now was sure - it was the ghost of Captain Tripp.

On our trip to Cove Island, we met a real light keeper, Jack Vaughan, who has the dubious honour of being the last light keeper on the Bay. Jack spent 24 seasons keeping the lights lit on these waters - the last 12 of which were spent at Cove Island. He was forced to retire in 1990 when the light station (the last one on the Bay) was auto-

Freighter in heavy seas

mated.

We spent an afternoon on Cove Island with Jack and his grandsons, exploring the three buildings (two residences and a machinery building) and the light tower he called home for so many years. Built in 1854, operations began in 1856. The Cove Island lighthouse quickly became one of the most important light stations on the Bay. It was the last reference point for vessels before the open water of Lake Huron. Every year, Jack would load up a half-a-year's worth of supplies and take a helicopter shuttle to the island to begin his solitary seven-month post. He lived in a house next to the lighthouse, and soon discovered he had neighbours - mice and rattlesnakes. But it was not until the resident bear introduced himself that Jack felt he had really met the Cove Island "welcome wagon." Part of Jack's daily routine soon involved feeding small cookies to a large bear, who would announce his arrival by pawing on the back door.

For some of his years at Cove Island Jack had a lighthouse assistant (not Captain Tripp.) Jack's wife and family visited on weekends and spent their summer holidays with him. When not busy with light keeper duties, Jack read through the boxes of books he always brought, tended his flower and vegetable garden, and landscaped.

Jack took us up the 114 stone steps inside the lighthouse to show us the view. He blew the old hand crank fog horn for us. The new one, located in the machinery building, operates on a 12-volt battery. More than a few birds took flight when we turned it on. Jack also showed us the original capstan marked with the initials C.W. (Canada West) dating from pre-confederation Ontario.

After twelve years on the Cove light, Jack Vaughan knows and respects the power of the Bay (especially after witnessing large rocks being tossed through the boathouse wall during a storm.) Due to his devotion, both 600-foot freighters with 18-foot (5.4-m) waves crashing over the bow, and small pleasure craft rendered immovable in dense fog could rely on the Cove Island light for guidance and reassurance. After retiring in 1991, Jack now lives in Tobermory repairing nets for commercial fishermen, and reading even more books. He is still watching the water, from the front window of his house overlooking Little Tub Harbour.

Other Cove Island Wrecks

Despite the light keeper's watchful eye and the light-house's powerful beacon, several wrecks can be found off Cove Island's shores. In addition to the *Regina* (see Cove Island story) and the *Charles Minch*, three unknown sailing ships lie off Cove Island's shores. One is just southeast of Gat Point. On the island's western shore about midway to Bass Bay are the remains of an unidentified sailing ship. You will find the front portion of her hull - about 60 feet (18 m) in length - lying among debris. *NOTE: The water is shallow - use a dinghy to access the dive site.*

On the island's eastern shore, adjacent to Boat Harbour, lies the second sailing ship on a sandy bottom in about 70 feet (21m) of water. Her sides are visible, and her rudder lies at about 50 feet (15 m). Just south of Cassel's Cove there is a third wreck in between 20-80 feet (6-24m) of water. This unidentified schooner is in three main pieces but quite broken up. The wreck is out from the Parks Canada sign for Cove Island.

Arabia Wreck

The 131-foot (39.3-m) barque the *Arabia* had made it through the gale of October 4, 1884, and was continuing the journey to deliver 20,000 bushels of corn to Midland. The only problem was the leak. As Captain Henry Douville pushed onwards, hoping to safely beach her, the crew spent hours pumping water out only to have it seep back in. In the early morning of the next day, even as Echo Island was drawing near, the captain had to order his crew to abandon ship. It was good timing. As they paddled their lifeboat to shore, the *Arabia*, after three decades of service and an Atlantic crossing, rapidly sank into 120 feet (36m) of dark, cold water.

One of the most inaccessible dive sites, it has perhaps the most to see. There are two buoys indicating her location - they lie just east of the wreck. Use the ropes to guide you down. Her largely intact hull lies at 110 feet (33m) with chains, bowsprit, windlass and bilge pump still present. Scattered around are spars, masts, running gear, her wheel and her steering mechanism. It is rumoured that when the *Arabia* was found years ago, her masts were still upright as if she was waiting to set sail again. *NOTE: Although her crew managed to escape, the Arabia has claimed the lives of more than one diver. The depth, strong currents, low temperature, and poor visibility combine to make this the most difficult and dangerous dive within the Park's boundaries. The dive should not be attempted unless it is under the direction of a dive master.*

Bears Rump Island
Marion L. Breck Wreck
Forest City Wreck

The dramatic limestone cliffs riddled with caves and precipices, and the powerful sound of the waves crashing against the shore on the eastern end of Bears Rump Island are impressive. This island had once provided sanctuary

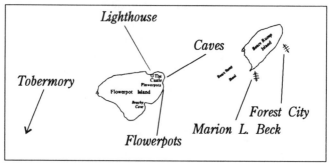

Refer to chart 2235

for the crew of the *Marion L. Breck*, one of the oldest ships to be wrecked in the Tobermory area. The date was November 15, 1900 and the schooner had just weathered a fierce gale in which her sails were torn, making her hard to manoeuvre. The wind and rough weather swept the ship towards Bears Rump Island where she ran aground on a reef. As the sun went down, the captain assured his wife (who was onboard for the final trip of the year) that everything was fine. They would abandon ship if necessary. As dawn broke, waves washed over the deck. The crew pumped furiously, but were finally forced to give up and take shelter on the island. Within hours, the ship broke up and slipped beneath the waves ending the career of one of the fastest lumber vessels on the lakes. Within a few days the lighthouse keeper from Flowerpot Island, Dan Smith, along with his two sons, rescued the stranded crew from Bears Rump Island.

The Breck's tragedy has created an interesting dive,

Forest City, foundered 1904

however. Bits and pieces can be found scattered in 5 to 100 feet (1.5 to 30m) along the shoal. Segments of her rigging and cargo can be seen among the rocks, a section of her hull is alongside the reef. Another section of her hull is at about 75 feet (22.5m), part of her keel lies in about 50 feet (15 m), and her capstan and an anchor are in shallower water. *NOTE: Do not be misled by the shallow parts of this dive. Like most of the dives in this area, it is for advanced divers only.*

June 5, 1904, Captain Humphrey of the *Forest City* was steaming west towards Lake Huron when a thick spring fog enveloped his 216-foot (64.8m) barge. Between Bears Rump Island and Flower Pot Island he misjudged his position, and struck the east end of Bears Rump Island. The ship's bow wedged itself among the shoreline trees. Captain, crew, and owner abandoned her and were saved by a tug from Tobermory. Attempts were made to salvage the *Forest City* but within two weeks, water broke through the bow. She filled and sank down an incline 60 to 150 feet (18 to 45 m).

While her forward section is quite broken because of the impact, the rest of the wreck is intriguing. The isolation, visibility, depth, and silence of this site play on one's imagination.

NOTE: This is a highly advanced dive. Divers have lost their lives exploring the wreck. Pay particular attention to depth as the incline can be deceiving.

Flowerpot Island

The flowerpots, magnificent rock pillars rising up on the island's eastern shore, remind you that this area has seen hundreds of millions more years than have we. While they are the feature attraction, the island has much more to offer. The park (part of Fathom Five National Marine Park) contains six beautiful and secluded campsites around Beachy Cove. Check with the Diver Registration Centre in Tobermory for details as the campsites are first come, first served. There are two docks in Beachy Cove, a smaller one for pleasure craft and a larger government dock for the Tobermory ferry. Interpretive materials point out the nature trails, and give information about the

Flower Pot Island

wildlife, plant life, and, of course, the flowerpots. A knowledgeable warden is on duty during the day.

The trail up the eastern shore leads to the flowerpots. It then heads into the cool interior woods past a small apple grove planted by a lighthouse keeper years ago. The trail continues to a viewing platform where Cabot Head and Fitzwilliam Island can be seen. Near the lighthouse the trail climbs up to a large cave one hundred feet (30 m) above the waterline, once used by a lighthouse keeper as his refrigerator. To enter the cave, you first must register by the main dock. Be sure to wear sturdy footwear, a hard hat and carry a flashlight.

Snorkeling or diving near the flowerpots is also a

treat, as there is just as fascinating a landscape underwater as above. Rocks, cliffs and underwater flowerpots make for wonderful exploring.

Vita Wreck

At 86 feet in length, the luxurious pleasure yacht, the *Vita*, was no match for the rough fury of Lake Huron and before long she was stuck on the shoal west of Yeo island. The year was 1910 and the owner, Frank Upton was entertaining a group of friends. They escaped unharmed, hair more or less in place, but the *Vita* was abandoned. The wreck is in 5 to 20 feet of water (1-6 m), west of Yeo Island just east of the Manitoba Ledge. A few interesting artifacts remain, including her propeller shaft. *NOTE: This is a very isolated part of the Bay pounded by huge waves crashing over the reefs. Choose a favourable day and take extra precautions.*

San Jacinto Wreck

Much can be learned while waiting in Little Tub Harbour for a boat to be fixed. In our quest for new material, new wrecks, new ghosts, we allowed our ear to be bent by a local fisherman/diver who told us about a newly discovered wreck north of the Fathom Five boundary: the *San Jacinto,* just off the northwest tip of Yeo Island (north of the *Vita* (see above) in 84 feet (25 m) of water. It was said to have sunk in 1896. The site was good: dead eyes, bilge

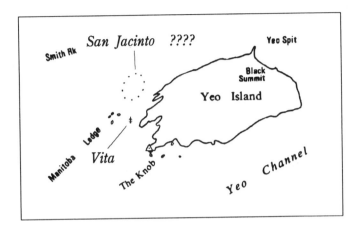

Refer to chart 2235

pumps, anchors and rudders were all visible. "There's a marker on it, you can't miss it," he assured us. So off we went. We found the marker, but the Bay's signature storm clouds were heading our way, and the site was too isolated for comfort. We switched on the fish finder to see if we could see its outline, but no luck. Maybe we were off-course, maybe the marker was marking something else, maybe we were close but not close enough... we did not find the *San Jacinto*. According to Karl E. Heden's *Directory of Shipwrecks of the Great Lakes*, the *San Jacinto* was a 265-ton vessel that foundered at the entrance to Georgian Bay on June 20, 1881, not 1896. This is all part of the Georgian Bay experience: mystery, tall tales, red herrings, new discoveries, and defeats.

City of Cleveland Wreck
S.D. Hungerford Wreck

The *City of Cleveland* has the honour of being the largest vessel to be lost in the Tobermory area. On its way to Midland from Lake Superior with 2,300 tons of iron ore in September 1901, this 256-foot (77-m) steamer was hit by heavy weather and driven onto a shoal west of Perseverance Island. Her crew was able to reach nearby Fitzwilliam Island, but the steamer quickly broke up along the rocks. Within days it was a complete loss. Lying in 10 to 30 feet (3 to 6 m) of water alongside the shoal, the *City of Cleveland* offers an impressive dive with her boiler, engine, massive 12-foot (3.6-m) propeller, and iron ore. The isolation of this wreck lends it a very haunted feeling especially on a stormy day.

Just north of the *City of Cleveland* is a point on the south end of Manitoulin Island named in honour of the *S.D. Hungerford*, a schooner wrecked near this location in November 1883. The *Hungerford*, laden with lumber, was being towed to Buffalo by the tug, the *Gladiator*. During a vicious gale, the *Gladiator* experienced mechanical problems and had to cut the tow line. The *Hungerford* broke up along the shore. The crew reached land, but had to endure the winter conditions for 19 days before being rescued. A small part of the wreck is located off Owen Island Bank in less than 15 feet (4m) of water. There are rumours that the rest of the wreck is close by in deeper water. If you have the time it might prove worth the search.

Manitoulin Island

On your way to the Bay's northern shores, you pass Manitoulin Island, the world's largest freshwater island - 94 miles (150 km) from east to west. Its eastern shore defines the northwest corner of Georgian Bay, but its main body stretches between Lake Huron and the North Channel. The beautiful eastern peninsula belongs to the Wikwemikong people of the Three Fires Confederacy of Pottawatomi, Odawa, and Ojibway tribes.   The Algonkian-speaking tribes who have inhabited this area for centuries believe that the good and evil spirits, Gitchemanitou and Matchimanitou live here; hence the name Manitoulin, or "dwelling place of the Great Spirit." The island boast an incredibly rich history - so rich it deserves its own book.

Fitzwilliam Island
Rattlesnake Harbour
Jenny Island

At the crack of dawn, the grinding sound of many boots on a pebble beach echoed across Rattlesnake Harbour. A handful of sleepy fishermen sailed out in their trusty Mackinaws (the fisherman's pick-up truck) to set their nets. Smoke curled up from the chimneys of the shanties, and the clanging of pots and pans could be heard. Children were roused from their beds to begin the day's chores. Across on Jenny, or Little, Island, the company

Refer to chart 2235

store opened for business; money was counted, nets were mended and tarred, the icehouse was cleaned to make room for the day's catch, and fish was prepared for pick-up by the *Hibou* (see p. 204). Another day at the Fitzwilliam fishing station had begun.

In 1901, Fitzwilliam Island was home to 26 families, all gathered on the shores of Rattlesnake Harbour on the northern tip of the island. There had been good fishing here since the late 1800s, an abundance of lake trout and whitefish to keep numerous families fed and clothed. The work was hard, and much of the fishermen's money went right back into the company store for supplies. But it was a good community, everyone helped each other, and there were plenty of campfires, fiddle-playing, and, on occasion, the imbibing of the fruits of someone's still. There were also frequent sailboat races with the fishermen from Squaw Island (see Squaw Island story in chapter three). Fishermen lived well for almost 50 years. After World War I, however, the number of fishermen at Fitzwilliam dwindled to about a dozen. By 1964, Fitzwilliam Island was silent.

Today Fitzwilliam's only inhabitants are some snakes of both the garden and Massasauga rattler variety. But don't let that deter you, the history preserved on this island deserves exploring. Wear rubber boots and pay attention to where you walk (not only to avoid snakes but also poison ivy.) Chances are the snakes will hear you coming and be long gone before you have a chance to cross their path. As you enter Rattlesnake Harbour by boat, you can see the roofs of seven buildings poking up through the trees and brush - one is a very old log cabin and the others

Fitzwilliam Island fishing camp

are frame houses and sheds. One structure has fallen into the water and been taken over by the beaver. Foundations, a few fire sites, and plenty of artifacts (bottles, cans, pots, etc. anywhere from ten to sixty years old) can also be found. There is even some bedding left in some of the bunkhouses.

Older artifacts can be found on Jenny Island, across from Fitzwilliam. Once the site of the company store, this small overgrown island is still the home to an almost-intact house, a collapsed structure that was probably the store, and a building that looks as if it might have been the icehouse. On exploring the shore, we found an old stove, a vat for tarring fish nets, and a rusty safe, no doubt once

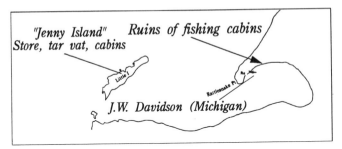

Refer to chart 2235

full of the earnings of the fishermen.

Because Rattlesnake Harbour was such a busy spot for Mackinaws, canoes, sailboats, numerous homemade "floating vessels" and steamboats, a goodly share of history remains below water, including four wrecks ideal for snorkeling over. Lying in about 10 feet (3 m) of water, adjacent to the abandoned fishing shanties, is the 180-foot (54-m) *J.W. Davidson* (sometimes referred to as the *Michigan.*) She and her tug, the *Harrison*, were a commonplace sight on these waters during the Bay's lumber boom in the 1920s and 1930s. In the southeast corner of the harbour there are other derelict vessels just beneath the surface. It is interesting to snorkel around the old dock site and look for artifacts - "junk" to the early residents.

When walking among the ruins of perhaps the most intact ghost town on the Bay, you can't help but let your imagination soar. Behind every door can be heard the welcoming voice of a fisherman's wife inviting you to taste her blueberry pie; along every path is an older brother clutching a garden snake in his dirty hand as he chases his terrified, shrieking younger sister; and along the shore where the dock once stood, there is a group of men discussing the day's haul, the sweet smell of pipe smoke mixing with the wet, fishy smell of the catch. This is Fitzwilliam Island.

Horse Island and Other Such Name Calling: The Alice Hackett Story

Fitzwilliam Island, so named by Admiral Henry Bayfield in honour of his mentor, Captain William Owen Fitzwilliam, was known for years as Horse Island. It earned that name as a result of the first-known wreck on the Bay, the wreck of the *Alice Hackett*.

In November, 1828, the British military post at Drummond Island was ordered closed and transferred to Penetanguishene. The *Alice Hackett* was employed to transport all the residents, supplies, and livestock from one base to the other. Quarters were cramped and the late November storm pitched the boat from side to side. One of the passengers, a tavern keeper by the name of Alexander Fraser had brought thirteen barrels of whisky with him. He had a brilliant idea: why not calm everyone's nerves with a wee nip o' whisky (and charge them of course.) Almost everyone keenly agreed, and soon the whisky was flowing. As the ship approached the Devil's Gap, the Captain, who had not been drinking, decided to beach the boat at or near Fitzwilliam and sit out the storm. Not a drinker, he was also not a gambler.

With the *Alice Hackett* securely aground, her crew

did their best to move the cargo to Fitzwilliam's shores, away from the pounding waves. They managed to save all the men, a barrel of pork, the tavern keeper and what was left of his 13 barrels of whisky. Only some of the freight, four horses, eight cows, twelve sheep, a few pigs, and the wife and daughter of one Monsieur Lepine were left on board. It seems Monsieur Lepine and the rest of the crew were so drunk they forgot about Lepine's wife, Angelique, and his baby daughter, Therise.

On the ship, Angelique and the baby huddled among the shifting freight. When a large cannon rolled into the hatchway and pierced a hole in the bottom of the vessel, Angelique decided it was time to seek higher ground. She tied Therise to her back and, in turn, tied herself to the mast. She hung on with all her strength, listening to the hammering of the waves and the screams of the terrified livestock, alternately praying to God and cursing her husband. The storm eventually broke and the men inevitably sobered up. Around 5 a.m. the next day, Monsieur Lepine remembered his wife and daughter. Not finding them on the island, he turned to look at the *Alice Hackett*. Whoops. A handful of contrite men went back to the Alice Hackett to retrieve Angelique and Therise, the only survivors other than a horse that had managed to swim ashore. He made the island his home, hence Horse Island. We do not know, however, how long after this incident Monsieur Lepine survived.

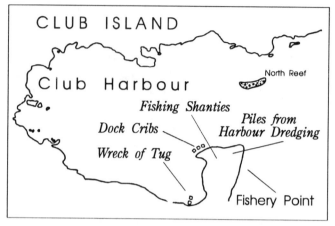

CLUB ISLAND

Club Harbour

North Reef

Fishing Shanties

Piles from Harbour Dredging

Dock Cribs

Wreck of Tug

Fishery Point

Refer to chart 2245

Lonely Island
Club Island Wreck

Lonely Island could have seen the end of John A. Macdonald, Premier of Upper Canada, and his political pals, on, coincidentally, July 1, 1859. They had boarded the side wheel steamer, the *Ploughboy* (see story page 53) for a trip up the Bay. All was going well until the Ploughboy broke the crosshead off her engine. The captain dropped anchor, and waited for another vessel to come by to help. Except for heavy waves, the horizon remained empty. The *Ploughboy's* anchors started to drag and she was carried closer and closer to the rocky shore of Lonely Island. It was time to act. Some crew members set

Fishing in Mackinaws

off to row all the way to Owen Sound in search of help. On the *Ploughboy*, the Speaker of the House of Commons was encouraged to say a few prayers. Someone must have been listening. As the ship was about to hit the rocks, her anchors caught and held. Soon after, a steamer appeared to rescue the group. They were happy to return to the capitol - by train.

As the name indicates, Lonely Island does not offer much for the boater. There is little shelter around the island, but its lighthouse, operating since 1879, is a valuable beacon on this stretch of open water. In contrast, Club Island to the west, with its protected harbour, is a popular layover. Club Island once sheltered a small fishing station, and can claim its own wreck in the southeast corner of the harbour close to the old fishing shanties and dock.

The day ends in a glowing sunset. As sailors and boaters nestle their craft into Club harbour, they sense the eloquence of Anna B. Jameson who, more than 150 years ago penned the words, "...sky like a bath of molten gold, the rock islands which studded its surface were of dense purple, except where their edges seemed fringed with fire. They assumed to the visionary eye, strange forms; some were like great horned beetles and some like turtles and, some like crocodiles, some like sleeping whales and winged fishes..." The worlds in which she and others - natives, missionaries, homesteaders, fishermen, shipbuilders, railroaders, loggers, cottagers and other adventurers - dwelt can only be imagined today. Their extraordinary experiences necessarily speak to those who travel Georgian Bay today. For us, they are the Ghosts of the Bay.

"Evening Calm" Geo Bay
—J.W. Bald

Picture Credits

Archives of Ontario:32, 35, 75, 87, 112, 114, 119,132, 137, 141, 151, 171, 172, 174, 177, 184,243
Bruce County Museum and Archives: 205,214,239,251
Cognashine Cottager:69, 78, 79, 80
Collingwood Museum:51, 52 , 158, 195, 205
Confederation Life Gallery of Canadian History: xvii,
County of Grey Owen Sound Musem:146, 201, 209, 231
Discovery Harbour:154
Grey Sauble Conservation Authority :225, 226
Huronia Museum:4, 29, 35 91, 97, 156, 159, 178, 196, 246, 272
Institute For Great Lakes Research:40, 44, 258,262, 267, 277
Metro Toronto Reference Library:xiv, 220, 222
M.T.L, Baldwin Room, John Ross Robertson Collection:xix,2, 13,18, 21, 29, 46, 53, 148, 187, 190, 265
Ministry of Natural Resources:47
National Archives of Washington:165
National Library of Canada: 286
National Archives of Canada:41, 58, 111, 121, 127, 182, 193, 197, 207, 270
Parry Sound Public Library:66, 67, 103, 106, 108, 109, 124, 126, 168
The Toronto Daily Star: 7, 23
University of Western Ontario, Regional Collection: 234

Private Collection

Lynx Images: 38, 49, 84, 93, 283, 293, 252, 279
Amelda Foley Archer: 63
Sandy Boyd and Elizabeth Boyd Andres: 98, 291

Selected Works for Further Reading

Amos, Art and Folkes, Patrick. *A Diver's Guide to Georgian Bay,* Ontario:
        Ontario Underwater Council, 1979.

Armitage, A. *Owen Sound: Steamboat Days*. Erin, Boston Mills Press, 1981.
        _____ *Owen Sound: The Day the Governor General Came to
        Town and Other Tales*. Cheltenham: Boston Mills Press, 1979.

Barry, James P. *Georgian Bay: The Sixth Great Lake*. Toronto: Clarke,
        Irwin & Co. Ltd., 1968.
        _____.*Georgian Bay: An Illustrated History*. Erin, : Boston Mills
        Press, 1993.

Bayfield, J. and Gerow, C. *This Was Yesterday: A Pictorial History of the Early
        Days of Penetanguishene*. Midland: Bayfield and Gerow, 1982.

Beaton, Horace L. *From the Wheelhouse: The Story of a Great Lakes Captain*.
        Cheltenham: The Boston Mills Press, 1979.

Bell, Rena. *A Peek in to the Past 100 Years: Midland 1878-1978*. Midland:
        Midland   Centennial Committee, 1978.

Boyer, D. *Ghost Ships of the Great Lakes*. New York: Dood, Mead, Co., 1968.

Bramah, Bill. *More Bill Bramah's Ontario*. Toronto, Cannonbooks, 1991.

Brazer, Marjorie Cahn. *The Sweet Water Sea: A Guide to Lake Huron's
        Georgian Bay*. Michigan: Heron Books, 1984.

Brown, Ron. *Ghost Towns of Ontario*. Toronto: Cannonbooks, Volume 1
        (1978); Volume 2 (1983);Field Guide (1990)

Bruce Trail Association. *Guide to the Bruce Trail,* Hamilton,,1992.

Callan, Kevin. *Killarney*. Erin, Ontario: The Boston Mills Press, 1990.

Campbell, William A. *The French and Pickerel Rivers: Their History
        and Their People*. Sudbury: William A. Campbell, 1992.

Cognashene Cottager, v.20 1967, v.22 1969, v.23 1970, v.30 1977, v.33

Cranston, J. Herbert. *Huronia.* Midland, Ontario: The Midland Press, 1951.

Croft, Melba Morris. *Tall Tales & Legend of Georgian Bay*. Owen
        Sound, Ontario: Melba Morris Croft, 1967.

_____*A Port of Some Importance: Owen Sound*. Owen Sound: Melba
        Morris Croft, 1984.

Dickason, O. *Canada's First Nations*. Toronto: McClelland &Stewart, 1992.

Fox, William S. *The Bruce Beckons*. Toronto: U. of Toronto Press, 1962.

Gateman, Laura M. *Echoes of Bruce County*. St. Jacobs: L. M. Gateman, 1982.

_____ *Lighthouses Around Bruce County*. Spinning Wheel , 1991.

Harrison, Gwen Smith (ed.). *A Pictorial History of Bruce CountyPrior to
        1918*. Port Elgin, : The Bruce County Historical Society, 1989.

Heden, Karl E. *Directory of Shipwrecks of the Great Lakes*. Boston:
        Bruce Humphries Publishers, 1966.

Jameson, Anna Brownell. *Winter Studies and Summer Rambles in Canada.*
        Toronto: McClelland & Stewart (NCL), 1990; originally 1838.

Kohl, Cris. *Dive Ontario!* Chatham, Ontario: Cris Kohl, 1990.

Macfie, John. *Now and Then*. Ontario; John Macfie, 1990.

_____. *Parry Sound Logging Days* Ontario: John Macfie, 1987.

Manly Steve. *Ports The Cruising Guide*, Ontario:Steve Manly, 1992.

McCuaig, Ruth. *Our Pointe au Baril.* Ontario: Ruth McCuaig, 1984.

Northcott, Bill. *Thunder Bay Beach*. Erin,: The Boston Mills Press, 1989.

Osborne, G.R. *Midland and Her Pioneers*. Belleville, Mika Pub., 1939.

Pearen, Shelley J. *Exploring Manitoulin*. Toronto: U. of Toronto Press, 1992.

Phillips, E.I. "The S.S. Midland", 1977.

Salen, R. *The Tobermory Shipwrecks*. Tobermory,:Mariner Chart Shop, 1985.

Sandell, Marion. *Keepers of the Light, Nottawasaga Island 1858-
        1983*. : Collingwood and District Historical Society, 1993.

San Souci & Copperhead Association. *Island Odyssey*. Ontario: San Souci &
        Copperhead Association, 1990.

Sims, James Percy and Preston, Mrs. C. *History of Wiarton and District*.
        Wiarton, Ontario: Percy and Preston, 1961.

PRIVATE PAPERS

Dave Thomas (Parry Sound) – "Vera Hay's Diary"

Boyd Andras, Elizabeth. "A little Bit Of Good Cheer", Toronto, 1972.

Jumbo Island" by Dorothy Bigger Klauder, 1985.

Index

Acknowledgements

The writers wish to express our sincere appreciation to those who helped make this project possible.

Erwin Abasamis, Elizabeth Boyd Andres, the Ashley Family, James Barry, John Birnbaum, Sandy Boyd, Peter Bowmar, Ron Brown, William A. Campbell, Barbara and R.W. Chisholm, Stephen Chisholm, T.A. Chisholm, Laura Cook, Craig d'Arcy, Mark Delvecchio, Luca Di Nicola, Bryan Drever, Sarah Duncan, Sheree Felstead, James Flaherty, the Flaherty Family, Nils Floren, Sean Gaherty, George & Antje Gutsche, Lois Harrison, Charles Harlton, John Hillis, Joan Hyslop, Jamie Hunter, Mary Kearney, Wally King, Marika Latorcai, Warren Lougheed, Trish Lyon, John Macfie, Brian Meisner, Morris Meneary, Scott Miller, Patricia Miscampbell, Nana & Papa, Karen Nichols, Glen Parr, Daryl Parr, Bill Phillups, The Pillgrem Family, Mr & Mrs Rudy Platzer, Brian Rhode, Louise Rhode, Elvino Sauro, Keith Sherman, Bill Smith, Ed Sluga, Dave Thomas, Laurine Tremaine, Sue Vanstone, Mrs. Vaughan (of Copperhead), Jack Vaughan, Rosemary Vyvyan, Nancy Westaway, Harry Whicher.

We also wish to thank the following institutions:

Georgian Bay Association, Secretary of State-Canadian Studies, Deptartment of Fisheries, Collingwood Museum, Huronia Museum, Discovery Harbour, West Parry Sound District Museum, Archives of Ontario, Public Archives of Canada, Canadian Coast Guard, Parry Sound Library, County of Grey Owen Sound Museum, Bruce County Museum and Archives, Baldwin Room at the Metropolitan Reference Library, Institute For Great Lakes Research.

ABOUT THE AUTHORS

Russell Floren, Andrea Gutsche and Barbara Chisholm are the three partners of Lynx Images, an unique company that combines filmmaking and book publishing as a means to explore and document vanishing pieces of Canadian history. Both *Ghosts of the Bay* and *Alone in the Night* are Canadian bestsellers.

Other titles from Lynx Images:

Superior: Under the Shadow of the Gods
Book & Video   ISBN 0-9698427-9-1

The North Channel and St. Mary's River:
A Guide to the History
Book   ISBN 1-894073-00-2

Enchanted Summers: The Grand Hotels of Muskoka
Book & Video   ISBN 1-894073-05-3

Alone in the Night: Lighthouses of Georgian Bay
Manitoulin Island and the North Channel
Book & Video   ISBN 0-9698427-4-0

Toronto: Stories from the Life of a City, Part 1: York
Video   ISBN 1-894073-03-7

All titles available at your local bookseller or from:
LYNX IMAGES INC.
PO BOX 5961, Station A
Toronto, Ontario M5W 1P4 Canada
Web site: http://www.lynximages.com